The PORSCHE 924/944 Book

The
PORSCHE
924/944
Book

PETER MORGAN

First published by
G. T. Foulis & Co. in 1990
Reprinted in 1998
Reprinted 2001, 2002 and 2006
by Haynes Publishing

British Library Cataloguing-in-Publication Data:
A catalogue record for this book is available from the British Library

ISBN 1 85960 864 7

Library of Congress catalog card No. 90-81744

Haynes Publishing, Sparkford, Yeovil, Somerset, BA22 7JJ, UK

Tel: 01963 442030
Fax: 01963 440001
Int. tel: +44 1963 442030
Int. fax: +44 1963 440001

E-mail: sales@haynes.co.uk
Web site: www.haynes.co.uk

Haynes North America Inc.,
861 Lawrence Drive, Newbury Park,
California 91320, USA

Typeset J. H. Haynes & Co. Ltd

Printed in Great Britain by
J. H. Haynes & Co. Ltd, Sparkford

C o n t e n t s

PORSCHE 924

Foreword

Good, helpful books on the Porsche 924 and 944 are few and far between.

It was with pleasure, therefore, that I received the invitation from Peter Morgan to pen a foreword to his book on the subject of these two water-pumping Porsche models which, for a while, were looked upon with some scepticism by the diehard rear-engine air-cooled 356 and 911 people!

Now accepted in all Porsche circles, both these models and their derivatives have been accorded respect on road and circuit. They are now firmly established in the Porsche Club Great Britain's Annual Concours event and in the Club's various Championship races.

I am sure that this informative book will allow Porsche 924 and 944 owners and prospective owners to be able to appreciate more fully the Porsche model of their choice and assist future owners to choose which particular type is the most suitable to their requirements. At the same time it will allow inspection and checking of the salient points to ensure a wise and safe purchase.

Roy Gillham
Executive Director,
Porsche Club Great Britain

Introduction & Acknowledgements

In 1979, when Professor Ernst Fuhrmann was chairman of the board at Porsche, he attributed the success of Porsche to a large degree to its unparalleled performance in competition. In a paper that was presented on his behalf to a conference at the Birmingham (UK) Motor Show that year, he stated that 'in 1950 the name Porsche was known, perhaps, to fifty engineers. Today, it is on the lips of every shoolchild'. The successes, in virtually every major international (and many national) motor sporting events throughout the world, have enabled the company to build up a strong following of loyal customers. It has also helped the development of their everyday vehicles. 'You don't have to race to build first-class cars, but the breakthroughs come quicker that way. It's rather like warfare ...' In just a few lines Prof. Fuhrmann summarised all that is Porsche.

Since the start of 924 production in 1976, that Porsche character has been reflected by the breathtaking pace of development. In the 924 Carrera series, the line has its own 'RS' equivalent, that can take its place alongside the best of the rear-engined classics that Porsche have previously produced. More recently, the 944 Turbo S has established itself as an outstanding high-performance car, which retains a practicality that Porsches have been noted for since the first 356.

This is a practical book, to help you get to know your front-engined Porsche and appreciate its excellence. The aim has been to present the background information needed to buy your car, then to discuss how its ever-increasingly complex systems work and how to approach problem diagnosis.

As well as a brief development history of the 924 and 944 models, there are sections on buying, the fuel and electrical systems, the engine types, suspension and body care. The book is completed by sections covering preparation for club competition and customisation. The comprehensive appendices include a full year-by-year specification section and production volume data.

The text has deliberately not covered detailed rebuilding sequences and for this information you are guided to the two Haynes Owners Workshop Manuals on the 924 (Bk No 397) and the 944 (Bk No 1027 US).

The 924 was born into an environment that could never accept second-best and when the decision was made to put the Porsche badge on its front, it was destined to become a classic.

Initially the front-engined Porsches were fairly rare at Club Concours events, but today the difficulty is keeping the class sizes at a manageable level, so that everyone stands some chance of success. The 924 and 944 have caught on with the enthusiasts in a big way and this is also shown by the number of knowledgeable people who were prepared to help me gather the information.

I have called on and pestered a great many people to get together all the data, including many friends within the Porsche Club Great Britain. In particular, I would like to thank the following: Bryan Walls, David Dickerson, Cliff Judd and Roger Watt, Melanie Hill, Corinna Phillips, Steve Kevlin of Porsche Cars (GB) Ltd, Roger Norris and Glenn Deering of Lancaster Garages (Colchester) Ltd, Chariots (St Albans) Ltd, Mark Scoles of Dick Lovett Ltd, Karen Dron (Gordon Bruce Associates for B.F. Goodrich), Mauro Andreini and Paul Smith of Tempo Racing, Richard Chilton and Mick Phillips of Club Automobiles Ltd, and Chris Turner. Final credit goes to my wife, Anne for lots of support during the preparation of the text.

Peter Morgan
Marlborough,
England.

CHAPTER 1
THE NEW DIRECTION

THE VW CONNECTION

Even before 1972 when Prof. Fuhrmann took over the running of the company, it made sound business sense to the company's senior managers to consider the concept of a new high-volume sports car that would combine the three characteristics of sportiness, practicality and economy. The new car would exist alongside the current relatively low-volume, high performance and luxury models, but the higher volume type would enable better continuity of profits and make the company less susceptible to fluctuations in the market. Even a small drop in demand for the 911 would place the company in a difficult position because of the large cost of the overall research and development activity.

Porsche's forward planning in the late sixties and early seventies had taken very seriously the progressive tightening of the US exhaust emission and noise standards. The US was the company's largest export market and it was clear that if a policy of expansion was to be maintained then major engine development would be required beyond the scope of the six-cylinder engine of the 911.

This thinking also coincided with a contract from Volkswagen to develop a successor to the VW-Porsche 914. The project, given the number EA425 was for development of a sporting

Ernst Fuhrmann, Chairman of Porsche AG from 1972 to 1981.

2 + 2, using a high proportion of VW and Audi components. The thinking was that the new car would be identified solely as a VW which, later, should the right conditions prevail, could be further developed into the new Porsche sports car, at less expense than starting from a clean sheet of paper.

Porsche's own earlier studies on future engine requirements had shown that a water-cooled engine was the only type to meet the forth-coming emission regulations. When it came to the configuration of the major components for the EA425, Porsche engineers aimed to give the car an optimum weight distribution for the type of car in prospect. For a 2 + 2 they figured a front-engined, rear-wheel-drive layout would work best, the limitations of front-wheel-drive being too much of a compromise for the enthusiasts at Porsche. The 2 + 2 requirement also eliminated a mid-engined layout. To improve the traction, rear wheel braking efficiency and, most importantly, the handling predictability, they suggested a transaxle arrangement with the gearbox and differential mounted at the rear. The first prototypes later showed that a well balanced 48 per cent front/52 per cent rear weight distribution had been achieved. When it came to the major components themselves, it was the four-cylinder engine from the Audi 100 that offered most potential from the then-current VW-Audi range. This was a single overhead camshaft 1984 cc design that was to be inclined at forty degrees in the new bodyshell. The engine was modified by using an aluminium crossflow cylinder head fitted to the standard cast-iron block and Bosch K-Jetronic fuel injection.

The transmission from the engine (and front-mounted clutch), comprised a drive shaft that ran back to

9

PORSCHE 924

The VW-Porsche 914.

changed the future of the new car was the oil crisis of 1973/74, which caused a serious fluctuation in sales for not only Porsche but all car manufacturers including VW. A change of leadership at VW at the beginning of 1975, and a subsequent review of their model policy, led them to cancel the new sports car, which was due to go into production later that same year.

Right: *This launch photograph of the 924 shows off its original clean lines.*

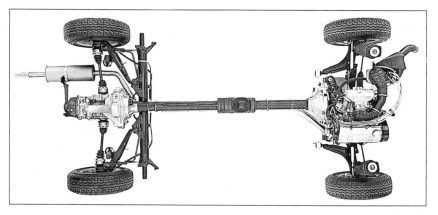

The major mechanical components of the 2-litre 924.

the gearbox/differential. The gearbox itself was initially to be an adapted four-speed Audi unit. Suspension and steering not surprisingly were mainly common VW or Audi parts. The front suspension used integrated Mac-Pherson-type spring/shock absorber units from the 1302 Beetle with the lower ends located by the lower wishbones from the Golf (Rabbit). At the rear Porsche chose to use the proven transverse torsion bar configuration seen on the 911, but again with many VW parts being used. Brakes were dual-circuit and servo-boosted to the disc front/drum rear layout.

No Porsche design proposal would be complete without consideration of the aerodynamics. It is in this area that Porsche were compelled to accept that their customer, VW, wanted styling for the market of the day, giving a product life of maybe five years. This timescale is typical for a large volume car in a highly competitive marketplace. If the design had been intended as a new model Porsche, then its profitability would have demanded a life of maybe ten to twelve years without major

restyling, the longer period being required to pay back the investment in new technology and tooling within a smaller annual production volume.

The result was an attractive design that achieved the lowest drag coefficient (C_d) of any contemporary passenger car, let alone a sports car. The designers managed to provide the desired 2 + 2 seating with a very large storage area for luggage, all in a bodyshell 78 mm shorter than the 911.

Porsche had progressed this design to the point that development was largely complete, with prototypes being evaluated and production tooling in progress. The wild card that

A NEW OPPORTUNITY

Porsche immediately saw the opportunity to take this almost production-ready car and add it to the current model range. A deal was completed with VW by the Spring of 1975 to buy back the design, with Fuhrmann trusting his design team's product and its market potential.

Porsche now set themselves a very ambitious launch schedule, which prevented any major restyling towards the ideal timeless shape previously discussed. The most important late decision was to use the hot-dip gal-

10

vanisation process that was to go into the 911 from the 1976 model year. This meant the 924 received, from its launch, the six-year anti-corrosion guarantee against rust perforation (in Europe). Another feature which now made the new car more appealing to the Porsche driver was the fitting of 911 seats although, happily, the dated instrumentation layout of the rear-engined car was not transferred and the 924 received a new contemporary interior.

The decision to market the new car as a Porsche made fast work necessary on the manufacturing side of the business, for there was not the capacity on the main Stuttgart/Zuffenhausen site to build the 924.

An early UK specification 924. Note the large headlamp washers.

PORSCHE 924

A compromise was necessary in manufacture which saw the production line set up in the closure-threatened VW plant at Neckarsulm, 25 miles from Zuffenhausen. The manufacturing agreement also saw Porsche complete the move to control the distribution of its cars by its purchase of VW's share of the joint VW-Porsche sports car sales company based at Ludwigsburg. Porsche had achieved an autonomous distribution network without damaging the good relationship with VW.

The first true 924 models were built late in 1975, with the first production series starting in January 1976. VW would build the new model under contract for Porsche. In order to meet Porsche quality standards the assembly at Neckarsulm was closely supervised initially by Zuffenhausen staff, but early standards did fluctuate.

The real problem was that some outsiders could not accept the new car was a real Porsche. This dismayed the engineers who had worked so hard on the project.

An understanding of the history of the Porsche name does serve to illustrate the reason for that dismay. Ever since his first vehicle, powered by hub motors, Ferdinand Porsche, then later his family and staff would address any technical problem by carefully assessing its components. With probably more emphasis than is healthy for most businesses, they applied the best engineering practice of having no preconceptions of the solution, until they had worked through the variables. This has been the practice for all of Porsche's products and was especially so of the 924. There was no 'standard' configuration for a Porsche. There was certainly no principle that said the engine had to be at the back or be air-cooled.

Sure, the 924 was not a winner in every department, as will be discussed shortly, but neither was the 911 initially. The two models may look very different, but the one thing they have in common is that they are without doubt both real Porsches.

ATTENTION TO DETAIL
The 924 wasn't going to set the world on fire, but with 125 bhp, the '76 European model could manage 124 mph and go to sixty in about ten seconds. It would even return 30 miles to the (Imperial) gallon. At the time, the car was noted for its lack of handling bad habits and, considering it was a sports car, the fact that it was superbly practical. There was room in the back for two pre-teenage children comfortably, with all the luggage space needed for a young family. It was not a 911, but it broke new ground as being the best value for money compared with any of the 'affordable' Porsche models from previous years. It also

A cutaway drawing shows how a practical 2 + 2 can be combined with a sports car specification. (Courtesy Autocar)

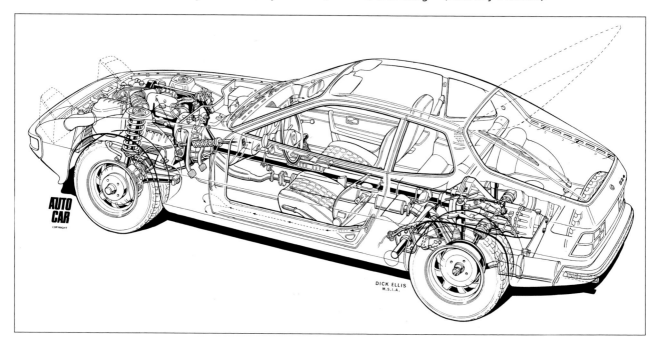

The 2-litre engine is inclined at forty degrees. Getting at the spark plugs, to the left of the camshaft cover, is difficult.

carried the Porsche badge at a time when the name had established itself as synonymous with success in competition.

In initial US specification, the car was definitely not a top performer (0-60 in 11.9 seconds and 111 mph top speed). All the US 924 models had exhaust gas recirculation and 'forty-nine'-state cars had air injection, with Californian cars getting catalytic converters. These statutory American additions effectively gagged the original 1984 cc engine, which struggled to develop a maximum 100 bhp (DIN)/95 bhp (SAE) at 5500 rpm.

Looking at a basic 1976 924 today, there is a feeling that somehow, something is missing. There is no large front air dam or rear spoiler, little external trim, basic steel wheels and no rear wiper. The engine is harsh and noisy and the four-speed Audi-derived gearbox uninspiring.

Even the exhaust tail-pipe seems unnaturally small.

The basic specification is given in Appendix 1, but that does not do justice to the attention to detail that the car was given by its engineers. This detail only became apparent when the car was taken beyond normal driving conditions. From the

beginning this Porsche was always comfortable and practical for either shopping or motorway cruising. The driver quickly accepted the lack of neck-breaking acceleration. Around town, the fuel consumption and slow-speed manoeuvrability were good. You didn't need fitness training to work the controls either. The car was just as at home on the open road, with a comfortable 80-100 mph cruise capability.

The good handling has been mentioned, but put the car on loose or snow covered surface and it was memorable! The 924 fired me up after an arm waving lock-to-lock session of pure fun one snowy winter in the hills around the Nürburgring. It showed off its pedigree in very difficult conditions, simply going where it was pointed until the front end broke away. What put the silly smile on my face was the way it would then come round by stepping on the throttle.

The interior of an early 924. Note the wind-up windows.

A 1976 924. The side repeaters and rear spoiler are later additions.

The stark rear threequarter view of the same 924, the spoiler helps as would the rubbing strips, fitted to more recent models.

There were faults with the early cars though, like the heating and ventilation. The heater seemed to be on all the time, not helped by a constantly idling fan. The combination of the large rear window and the unstoppable warmth from the heater made life uncomfortable on even moderately cool days. There were not many early 924s driving around that did not have their driver's window open an inch, to let cool air in! This poor system was to dog all 924, 924 Turbo and early 944 models, until the 'oval' dash made its entry in 1985.

PRESS REACTION

In July of 1976 *Road & Track* had compared the 924 to the Alfetta GT and the Datsun 280Z and voted the German car the winner, even in its original 100 bhp form. It is easy to be cynical and say that the 924 should have been the better car, because it was $3000 more than the 280Z and $1000 more than the Alfa. The 924 had to be technically better to survive in this market. They made the point that the big feature the 924 had over its predecessor, the

914, was that the newer car was far better looking. It was the hard-core Porsche fans that were levelling the comments that the car was slow and expensive, even when the figures showed that as a replacement for the 912 and 914, it was a superior performing car, especially in its handling. The engineers at Weissach were not taking these criticisms lightly, even when the sales figures showed that the 924 was turning into Porsche's biggest selling car ever. These good sales were coming from customers who were not the hard-core Porsche Club types who only worshipped the 911, but the broader sports car enthusiast who turned to the 924 because it was simply a better value package than anything else in its class.

The press generally did catch on to Porsche's stated objective that the 924 was a sports car for the eighties, where neck-breaking performance would not be the overriding factor and where comfort, good road manners and fuel efficiency would be important. It still was in every sense, though, a full sports car.

The road reports praised many of these factors, especially the good handling, but they continuously came back to the shortcomings of the engine which they rated as too rough and noisy for its class. Right from the 924's launch, performance comparisons began to be made with the faster mass production saloons. Sometimes the comparisons were not too flattering to the Porsche. The criticisms about the engine noise and smoothness betrayed its Audi heritage and would only eventually be settled by the introduction of Porsche's own engine in 1982.

The styling came in for mixed review as well. The drag coefficient for the new car was outstanding at 0.36 (in 1979 the 924 Turbo achieved 0.34, the lowest European production car Cd of the time). It was felt generally that the car was very elegant. Some found the rear three-quarter view difficult to live with and that aspect was certainly improved by the later addition of a small spoiler around the lower edge of the opening rear window. Unfortunately, that made the rearwards visibility worse when parking or reversing. The smooth shape had resulted in a large glass area at the rear which, although fine for the North European climate, made life unbearable inside the car anywhere there was prolonged hot weather. For these climates air conditioning became essential.

It was in its country of origin that the 924 had the hardest time from the press, who after examining all the early car's faults and then its price, wondered loudly whether the car was good enough to be called a Porsche.

In the States, too, some customers were asking why they had to pay extra for such luxury car basics as alloy wheels, headlamp washers, rear wiper and passenger door mirror. It was necessary to have most of the options to make the car practical and this, combined with early price increases made the car expensive compared with its (especially Japanese) competition.

Despite these criticisms, the car was publicly well received and sales began to accelerate at a rate never seen before by Porsche.

It was accepted by most industry observers that a few years would be required before the detail criticisms would be overcome. Attention at Weissach was now fully concentrated on making what was a good basic design much better. Professor Fuhrmann had no difficulty in approving a stream of improvements, now that the car was in the market and beginning to show a return. These developments also served to show Porsche's commitment to improve the new car. Sales were remarkable. The 50,000th car was delivered in April 1978 and the 100,000th by February 1981. Such a result turned out to be a happy retirement present for Fuhrmann and a total justification of the

high risk decision to buy the project from VW in 1975. He had seen the 924 become the most successful car in volume terms that Porsche had ever built. He had certainly set it on a development path that initially led to the 924 Turbo and then the company's own-design 2.5-litre engine. Fuhrmann was succeeded as Porsche Chairman in January 1981 by Peter Schutz.

924 DEVELOPMENTS

The first update for the 924 came in February 1977, halfway through the model year. The improvement was only for the breathless US model with power being increased to 110 bhp SAE. This was achieved by raising the compression ratio to 8.5:1, new camshaft timing and fitting 40 mm intake valves. The US spec cars started with 38 mm valves even though all other versions used 40 mm from launch. The rear axle ratio was changed and all now had catalytic converters (with Californian cars also getting the air injection).

In Europe, a three-speed automatic

transmission had been available since late 1976, but it was not until March 1977 that it was offered to the States. There was a top speed penalty, too, which reduced the performance still further, but it did offer two-pedal 924 driving for those that wanted it. Bryan Walls, Editor of *Porsche Post* (the magazine of the Porsche Club G.B.) wrote in 1982 of his experiences with an automatic European spec 924. He noted that the 924 was hardly a road-burner and that it never got his adrenalin running, except when he pulled out to overtake while going up a hill and nothing happened! Automatic US spec cars with the 110 bhp SAE engines would go to sixty in 12.8 seconds, against an official 10.4 seconds for a manual European car.

The factory produced a series of 'World Champion' 924 models, painted in the style of their then-current Martini-sponsored racing cars.

The three-speed automatic further reduced the already mediocre performance, especially on US models.

Above: *Sound-deadening material fitted to the bonnet of this 1978 model 924.*

Left: *This late 1978 model shows the wipers on the 'wrong' side for this RHD model, giving a blind spot to the right of the driver's eyes.*

The same 1978 model from the rear, showing the oval exhaust, introduced the previous year, and rear wiper, again on the 'wrong' side for RHD.

They are identifiable by a special dash plaque. This was the first sign that the 924 was beginning to move away from its originally intended market position as an entry-level model.

The September 1977 Frankfurt Show saw the introduction of the optional five-speed transmission. This was good news except that first gear was on a 'dog-leg' to the left and back of the normal H-pattern. It provided a real fifth gear, not an over

drive, so that it was easier to keep the engine in the maximum torque range, between 3000 and 5000 rpm. The pattern was fine for racing, where first gear might only be used at the start, but get the car in a slow moving traffic line in town and the difficult selection of first gear quickly became a pain.

The 1978 models showed little change over the 1977 range, except the usual colour variations externally and internally. The improvements to the noise level continued and the car was given a revised exhaust system, notable for its large oval (and chromed) tailpipe. The release literature promised that electric windows and powered external door mirrors (first seen on the 911) would be available 'at a later date'. Frustratingly, the windshield wipers had still not been

A 1979 model. Note the chequer board upholstery.

repositioned for right-hand drive versions. This was almost excusable for the early models, but this important safety feature for RHD cars turned out to be neglected through the whole life of the 924.

The Getrag pattern five-speed gearbox became standard for the 1979 models. The original four-speed Audi item was discontinued, to many sighs of relief, the Audi synchromesh having never been liked by Porsche's staff or their customers. An easy way of differentiating between a 1979 model and earlier types is the cloth inserts in the door panels of the later model.

This was the first year that the 'Space-Saver' tyre was used. This method of providing a means of getting the driver home was and still is an unpopular solution to punctures. The space-saver was not permitted legally in Britain initially, but was used from 1979 in all Porsche's other markets.

There were several key changes for 1980. Most visible inside the car was the introduction of the chequerboard velour interior trim. The more conservative plaid could still be specified. The two-tone finish seen on the 924 Turbo launched in early 1979 could be ordered on the standard 924. This year also saw the black rubbing strip introduced on the sides together with the opening cap for the fuel filler.

The latter was a very acceptable styling improvement for what was now a relatively expensive car in its performance class.

The dog-leg first gear disappeared on the standard 924, with the fifth gear now being up and to the right of the 'H'. European models also took the step up to transistor ignition during 1980 (not to be confused with the later digital electronic ignition).

If you own an early 924 model, you may be aware of the hot start problem that could affect these cars. It has always been difficult to restart a warm engine after shut-down. A strong battery is essential and the driver can sit there churning the motor for a long time without the

PORSCHE 924

engine firing. Pausing makes no difference. The problem was fixed in two stages with 1980 models having better start enrichment and an extra, tank-mounted, fuel pump. This was followed in 1981 by the fitment of a one-way valve after the main pump. This made all the difference and reduced the embarrassment of failing to start the car. From 1980 an oxygen sensor was fitted in certain markets where emissions control was required. This simple device, linked to the Bosch K-Jetronic system, enabled more accurate monitoring of the air/fuel ratio. This meant better combustion efficiency and exhaust emissions. The oxygen sensor is fitted on the exhaust manifold and its function is described later.

During 1980, the six-year guarantee for the lower body was extended to seven years and the cover expanded to include the whole bodyshell. The guarantee was against rust perforation, which officially meant 'rust-through damage to body parts'. The earliest 924 models only had hot-dipped zinc-coated floor pans. From 1978 only the roof was not zinc coated, but the following year the whole bodyshell was fully zinc coated. In the UK the new seven-year guarantee was conditional on annual inspection by an Official Porsche Centre. Any unauthorised crash or paint repair would invalidate the guarantee. In the US there was no requirement for regular inspections after sale. The guarantee was a factory contract which could pass from owner to owner and was an up-front statement about the high production quality levels being achieved by the company.

The press releases for the new 1981 models made much of the effort that had been put into noise reduction. The handling was improved, too, with the front anti-roll (stabiliser) bar becoming a standard item. In the US this was combined with stiffer rear torsion bars to give

Above: *This 1985 924 has the optional 'Turbo' alloy wheels fitted with 205/60 R15 tyres.*

In its last model year, 1985, the 2-litre 924 had tinted glass as standard and 'telephone dial' wheels.

improved cornering. The previously available 'M' sports suspension option was therefore discontinued. The major improvement for the American cars that year was the standard fitting of four-wheel disc brakes, a feature the European 2-litre 924 was never to see.

The Frankfurt Show of 1981 signalled the end for the Audi-engined

924 in the US where the 944 replaced it and the 924 Turbo. In Europe, where the 924 was more popular, it continued with minimal change. The 1982 models featured a 12,000 mile service interval (although the oil was still to be changed every 6,000 miles). It received the 924 Turbo steering wheel and a Porsche crest on the glove compartment latch.

The small car rear lip spoiler fitted to the 1983 models gave the 924 an excellent 0.33 drag coefficient and certainly improved the rear-end looks. By 1984, with over 130,000 cars sold worldwide, the 924 was into its ninth year. Development was slowing considerably, but detail changes were still being introduced. The notable new gadgets that year included the electrically tilting sunroof, which was also removable. Another feature was the electric release for the rear opening window. The switch for this was located inside the passenger compartment. Also inside was new cloth trim for the seat inlays, with the Porsche name woven into the fabric. The seat back release was also revised. The difficult-to-clean 924 Turbo wheels, which now could be specified as an option, came with locking wheel nuts.

Within the car business, one of the recognised tactics to give a model a sales boost as it goes past its peak popularity is to load it with previously optional features. By 1984, the press had detected this treatment on the 924 and rumours were circulating that maybe the 924 was about to be chopped.

Official comment was a tight-lipped response that the 924 was not about to be discontinued. The 1985 models, announced in September 1984, again offered only detail changes (like tinted glass). However, it was the engine, not the car, that

was threatened and in April 1986, the 924 became the 924S. The 924 had taken on the new 2.5-litre engine first fitted to the 944.

924S

There had been many customers who preferred the smooth lines of the 924 over the more aggressive look of the 944. It was this factor, more than any other that had sustained sales of the 924 after the 944 was launched in 1982. Just a year after that launch, 944 production volume had reached 24,761, whilst the 924 (now not sold in the US) had dropped to 5,887 units. The 1984 rumours about the death of the 924 had some foundation in logistics. Supplies of Audi's short engines, particularly the cast-iron block, were expected to be discontinued by 1986. The block was no longer used in any VW/Audi model and Porsche volume alone was not enough to be economic. Combine this with the ever-present criticism from a loud minority that the car was a cheap, noisy and under-powered Audi with a Porsche badge on the front and a decision could have rationally been made to discontinue the car completely.

In my view that is what should have happened. It would have been completely justifiable to continue to supply the demand for the Audi-engined 924 until such time as engine supplies were threatened and then retire the car gracefully. Of course, it is very easy for an outside observer to make comments like this without being fully in the picture, particularly with regard to the balance sheet. It was probably the financial fact of life, combined with spare capacity, which prompted Porsche to attempt to give the 924 a new start.

The upgrade was, of course, obvious. To the long-time 924 fan, the

press reaction was predictable: 'Lily-livered 924 grows up!', 'A real Porsche at last!', 'Stuttgart's baby gets the power it always wanted!'

The 2.5-litre 944 engine was detuned from 163 bhp (DIN) to 150 bhp by lowering the compression ratio from 10.6:1 to 9.7:1. This was achieved by deepening the dish of the piston bowl, rather than changing the cylinder head. This allowed the 924 to run on 2-star fuel. To be fair to the 924, it did have another 25 bhp more than previously, with more torque as well. In the UK's *Motor* magazine 135 mph and a 0-60 time of about 7.8 seconds had been achieved. That was a big improvement. The factory figures were 133 mph and 8.4 seconds. One was reminded, though, that this same magazine had recorded a time to 60 mph in just 8.2 seconds with a 1977 preproduction 2-litre model, when later production-line examples averaged about 10.5 seconds. The reason for this, it was later learned, was that Weissach had built the original preproduction 924s used for press testing!

Normally one would tend to believe a magazine road report, but in this case the Porsche figure may be more believable as a true representation of the average model. Either way, the 924 now had really good performance. The chassis was mostly 924 Turbo, without the NACA duct and front spoiler slotting, but with ventilated disc brakes all round and the option of sports anti-roll bars and shock absorbers. The 924 retained its (smaller) rear spoiler, not getting the larger 944 version and used the 'telephone dial' wheels. The stiffer cast rear suspension arms from the 944 range were also fitted. Unfortunately, the new 'oval' dash was not fitted to the 924S, which is surprising as the old three-hole version was looking

PORSCHE 924

Right: *The 'S' added to the rear logo was the only obvious external change for the new 2.5-litre model.*

Below: *The new 924S retained the original 'three-hole' dash. Now where is that headlamp switch?*

Below right: *Attractive artwork marks one of the 37 limited edition black 'Le Mans' models sold in the UK during 1988, the 924's final year.*

distinctly plain by now. The old problem remained of having to peer around the steering wheel to look at some of the gauges and switches.

The new 924 was relaunched in the US, with identical power with the European 924S, even though a catalytic converter was fitted to the former. The two models differed only in their microprocessor chip that mapped engine performance. The car went well, but it was poor value for money compared with its competition. It was now perceived as a down-market 944, which was progress indeed from the earlier accusations that the car was not even a 'real' Porsche. Customers were not

impressed by the basic fit of the 924S though, the model lacking the passenger door mirror and even wiring for a radio. It was far too expensive to be classed as an entry-level model, but was too basic to stand alongside the other Porsche models.

The 924S could not be classified as a success in 944 terms or even when compared with the original 924. The 924S was discontinued in August 1988, after only two and a half years in production.

924 TURBO

Ever since the 917 Can-Am racers had blown the opposition into the weeds during the 1972/3 seasons,

Porsche had been highly respected for their understanding of turbocharging technology.

Turbocharging is the process whereby a small fan or turbine placed in the exhaust stream is used to drive another turbine placed in the air induction system. This results in the induction air being compressed and a greater mass of air/fuel mixture being delivered to the combustion chamber during each induction stroke. The higher density of charge thus available means more energy is available to push down the piston. In short there is more power for a given combustion chamber volume.

Porsche had achieved 1100 bhp

from the Can-Am car and had very successfully raced turbo cars since. The depth of their expertise was shown by the launch of the 911 Turbo in 1974, demonstrating that a turbocharged road car could be both exhilarating to drive and reliable.

This early 924 Turbo shows off the two-tone paint finish and 'new' rear spoiler.

The 924 Turbo, introduced in 1979, was priced well beyond the standard 924. Left-hand drive versions were on sale from early 1979 and British right-hand drive versions from October 1979. The British five-speed 924 Lux cost £9,582 at that time, with the Turbo selling for £13,629. What many did not realise, however, was that this was not just another add-on turbo conversion. The Weissach engineers had gone over the whole car, modifying anything which was considered to be of marginal specification. Their efforts produced an outstanding car.

The Turbo engine was not built at Neckarsulm, but at the main Zuffenhausen Porsche site. 'Short' engines (the block, crankshaft, pistons and connecting rods) were trucked from Neckarsulm so that a newly designed cylinder head could be fitted. After assembly, inspection and a demanding running-in test cycle, the engines were trucked back to Neckarsulm for final assembly.

The standard 924 Audi head was of the Heron type, that is completely flat, with the valves operating vertically in line with the piston movement and with no angular displacement. The pistons were therefore dished to prevent valve contact.

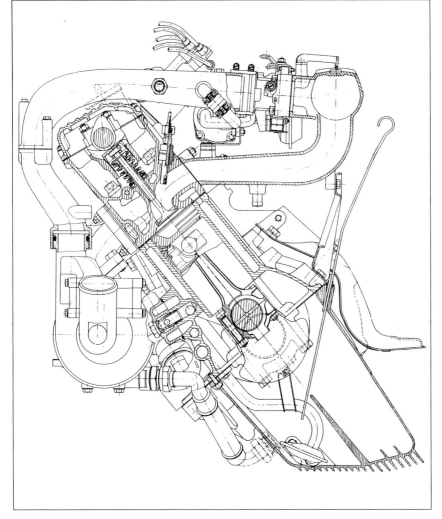

Section through the 924 Turbo engine, showing recessed cylinder head volume.

The KKK turbocharger, showing the exhaust turbine.

The Turbo still had the dish in the (now forged) pistons, but the new cylinder head used a different combustion chamber layout with a recessed volume. This lowered the compression ratio, necessary to prevent detonation, but at least allowed a longer travel on the valves. Skinned knuckles were a pain of the past, since the plugs were relocated to the induction side of the new head.

The KKK (standing for Kuhnle, Kopp & Kausch) turbocharger was sized to become effective at relatively low engine revs, with the maximum boost of 0.7 bar (one bar equals one atmosphere or 14.7 psi) being effective at 2800 engine rpm. The turbo itself reached a maximum speed of approximately 100,000 rpm. The engineers claimed that a boost gauge was unnecessary, since they had put so much effort into making the cut-in effect of the turbo very smooth. Luckily for the driver they didn't fully succeed and that firm push in the back from about 2,500 rpm could put a smile on most faces! The boost gauge would have been appreciated by most customers, if only as a conversation starter! The smoothness was possible by using, firstly, a wastegate to limit the boost pressure in the system. This was located on the exhaust side of the turbo and

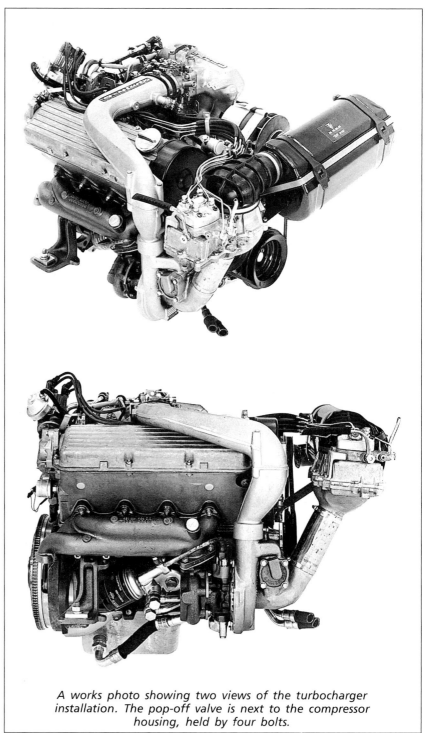

A works photo showing two views of the turbocharger installation. The pop-off valve is next to the compressor housing, held by four bolts.

dumped excess exhaust gases directly into the silencing system (or catalytic converter) when the pressure in the intake manifold exceeded 0.7 bar. On US models the wastegate protected the converter from very hot exhaust gases. The second feature was a pop-off valve located across the intake and exhaust sides of the turbo housing. This reduced the so-called throttle lag, a flat spot effect noticeable when accelerating hard after a period of closed throttle, for instance when coming out of a tight bend. The closed throttle resulted in a pressure build-up in the intake side which slowed the exhaust turbine. When the throttle was opened, the turbine speed would take time to speed up again, which showed as a lag in acceleration. The pop-off valve bled the intake pressure into the exhaust side and maintained the turbine rpm against the closed throttle, which meant a less noticeable throttle lag. US versions used a slightly smaller diameter turbo, which helped reduce the lag effect. The minimum lag achieved was the best achievable in the late seventies but, such is the pace of development, it would be considered poor today.

Ignition was still of the transistor type, with rev limiting. The Bosch K-Jetronic Continuous Injection System (CIS) was adjusted to suit the larger air volumes involved. A second fuel pump was fitted to enable a higher system pressure, a modification which was passed on to the standard 924 the same year, as a contribution to solving that car's hot-start problem.

The Turbo received a separate oil cooler, whilst air flow over the hotter-running engine was increased by the addition of additional slots in the front spoiler and front panel between the headlamps, together with a sleek and fashionable NACA duct in the bonnet. A flexible spoiler below the

The 924 Turbo can easily be distinguished by the additional cooling slots and the NACA duct in the bonnet.

engine lower shield increased the cooling flow further by causing a low pressure area under the engine. This helped front brake cooling also.

The engine stayed at 1984 cc, but power went from 125 bhp (DIN) for a standard European 924 to 170 bhp with the new Turbo. Torque was 180 ft lb (previously 121.5 ft lb). In the US the equivalent change was from 110 bhp (SAE) to 143 bhp (SAE), with a maximum torque of 147 ft lb (from 111 ft lb). Apart from the cooling modifications to the front panels, a Turbo could be identified by the flexible rear spoiler fitted to the opening tailgate and the new spoke-effect alloy wheels. It was a very attractive package, which showed how little need be done to the 924 to make it a real head-turner. The driveshaft to the gearbox was increased in diameter from 20 mm to 25 mm but unfortunately the five-

speed transmission kept the Getrag pattern with its 'dog-leg' first gear. The half-shafts were strengthened and ventilated disc brakes were fitted to the rear hubs of European cars. The wheels used five studs rather than the four-stud fixing of the then-current 924. There were stiffer springs, revised anti-roll bars and stiffer shock absorbers. The lower body, less roof section, now carried a six year anti-corrosion guarantee.

Press reaction was euphoric. *Road & Track* made the 924 Turbo its 1000th road test in June 1979, giving the new model a well-earned place of honour for this special anniversary. Testing an American spec 924 Turbo around a snow-covered Weissach, they achieved 0-60 mph in just 7.7 seconds.

This was only 0.7 seconds slower than a 3-litre 911SC; and the two cars shared a top speed of 140 mph! The Weissach engineers must have known also how enjoyable *R&T* would find the 924 Turbo's superior handling on the snow-covered roads around the Development Centre. The

testers noted that the buzzy noise of the standard 924 had been replaced by a lower frequency, softer engine note and that there was a significant increase in sound-deadening material. They noted the exhilarating whistle from the turbo as it wound up. You could have a lot of fun playing racing drivers, by anticipating the power-on point in bends and trying to get the boost up early for a quick exit from a corner.

The 1981 model (also known as the Series 2) was significantly improved with an extra 7 bhp and a claimed 14 per cent better fuel consumption. Top speed rose to 143 mph and the 0-60 time fell to 7.5 seconds. The key difference was the adoption of the Siemans-Hartig digital ignition system. This was the first engine-management computer used on a production Porsche and it permitted the compression ratio to be increased to 8.5:1 without risk of engine knock. The technicalities of engine management will be explained further in the 944 chapter. What the press releases didn't men-

tion was that the crankcase breathing had been modified to give better oil circulation after engine shutdown. This was aimed at extending turbo life, which had been found sometimes to be very short when the car was used hard. The cause was turbo bearing and seal wear, a problem not to be satisfactorily solved until the 944 Turbo was introduced in 1985. The 1981 European models used a slightly smaller turbo to improve lower speed flexibility. These improved 1981 models can easily be identified by the side repeater flashers ahead of the doors.

The 1982 models were unchanged technically, being identified by carpeted door pockets and the option of forged 'telephone dial' wheels.

The 944 was launched in the UK on 1 July 1982, left-hand drive models having become available from early 1982. Outside Europe, that spelt the end for the 924 and 924 Turbo. It wasn't the intention to stop production of the 924 Turbo immediately, but the rapid success of the 944 meant that the hard decision

had to be made early because there was only so much capacity at Neckarsulm. The 1983 model, announced in August 1982, did not include the 924 Turbo, although stock continued to be sold into the Italian market until early 1984.

The turbo ducting is the most obvious difference in the engine compartment. Note also the fuel metering unit is now on the right side.

924 CARRERA GT

Of all the 924 and 944 models produced, the Carrera GT is the one which is the most desirable. It has the advantage of being a limited production model (only approximately 400 were made) and it has a racing pedigree. The romance was generated by Porsche's performance at Le Mans in 1980, when three Carrera GT models came in sixth, twelfth and thirteenth. They were all works entries, but financed by the Porsche organisations of Germany, USA and Great Britain. It was a great achievement against the might of the 935 types that were dominating sports car racing at the time. The British car's finish was especially sweet for its drivers Andy Rouse and Tony Dron, who were well known within their home racing circles, but not given any hope in the twenty-four hour classic. They made it to the finish despite Dron losing the entire nose section at one stage, after being caught in the turbulent slipstream of a passing 935 on the Mulsanne straight and then driving for the last five hours on three cylinders, because of a burnt exhaust valve. The same problem affected the American entry for Holbert/Bell, but the German car of Barth/Schurti ran virtually fault-free throughout.

As proposed at the Frankfurt

An unpainted prototype 924 Carrera GT. Three of these cars finished sixth, twelfth and thirteenth in the 1980 Le Mans.

Motor Show in September 1979 (where else!), the concept 924 Carrera GT was a highly developed version of the 924 Turbo. It was said that it was a model suitable for racing and could be produced in figures suitable for homologation into Group 4 racing for 1981 and eventually the proposed Group B that would start in 1982. The concept car was developed into the limited production version launched in June

1980. It took very little further modification to produce a highly competitive racer and, in fact, two versions were offered from the start. There was the relatively well equipped (and road-legal) limited production run of 400 models of the standard GT, which was the homologation special. The second version was the 'Le Mans' model, which actually was the proposed Group 4 racer and this latter version was the basis for the factory cars at Le Mans in 1980.

The standard GT used the 924 Turbo engine, which with the addition of an air-to-air intercooler (fitted

over the top of the engine) and many other detail modifications produced 210 bhp at 6000 rpm.

Porsche have always had a talent for weight reduction. The company could draw on experience that covered the whole history of the marque, starting with the lightweight 356 models of the fifties, the 'Bergspider' hillclimb cars of the sixties and the lightweight 911 racers of the seventies. It was no surprise that the Carrera GT was 400 lb lighter than the standard 924 Turbo. This remarkable reduction was achieved mainly through the use of thinner sheet steel and aluminium doors and

25

bonnet. There was an aluminium transaxle tube and lightened suspension components. Bilstein shock absorbers were fitted and the springs were stiffened, which gave a firmer ride. The front spoiler, front wings and the rear wheel arch extensions were made of glass-filled flexible polyurethane.

An air-to-air intercooler was fitted into the ducting between the turbo and the air distributor.

The 245 bhp Carrera GTS.

Inside, the lightening process was continued with simplified fittings and lightweight seats. The approach to the whole car was identical to that taken with the RS Carrera 911 in 1972/3 and the Carrera GT reflects the same purposeful character. The combination of the improved engine output and the lighter weight gave the Carrera GT supercar performance with a quoted factory top speed of 'over 150 mph' and a 0-62 mph (ie 0-100 km/h) time of 6.9 seconds.

Two more variants were announced in March 1981, following completion of the homologation-run of 400 GT models. At the time it was claimed these later cars were an 'evolutionary' series of pure competition cars, although quite a few were equipped for road use.

The Carrera GTS produced 245 bhp by using a maximum turbo boost of 1.0 bar. The engine also showed better low speed torque than the GT. These improvements enabled a 0-62 mph time of 6.2 seconds and a top speed of 155 mph. The suspension was uprated, including lighter front wishbones and coil spring rear suspension with cast aluminium trail-

ing arms. The brakes all-round were ventilated and cross-bored discs and used 911 Turbo hubs. It weighed 2472 lb (1121 kg), which compares with 2602 lb (1180 kg) of the GT. This car was fully road legal but was given lighter weight equipment than the GT, using glass-fibre bonnet, doors, wings and rear bumpers. A 'very few' GTS models were specified with full interiors, with wind-up windows replacing the sliding Resard plexiglass side windows. These had 911 seats in place of the 935 items and a glass tailgate with wiper in place of the basic plexiglass. One owner even specified a full leather interior.

For use by privately entered teams the GTS could be specified in pure race or rally forms, with further modification from the GTS. The Rally version produced 280 bhp and came with greater ground clearance, stronger suspension, underbody protection and roll- over bar.

The ultimate 924 Carrera version was the GTR, derived from the original 'Le Mans' model of 1980. The GTR was a pure racer and weighed a mere 2084 lb (945 kg). The heavily

modified 2 litre engine, still able to claim an Audi heritage, produced 375 bhp. Amongst the many changes, Kugelfischer mechanical fuel injection was used and the larger turbo was relocated on the left-hand side of the engine block. To stop this projectile, the brakes from the 917 were used (which had been further developed on the 935 series). The press release for the GTR blandly stated that 'this should assure private owners in the Group 4 category of good results in the 1982 World Endurance Championship'. It certainly wasn't cheap, costing £34,630 in the UK in December 1981 (against £9103 for a 924 and £19,000 for an equipped Carrera GT). Apart from the prototype which was painted white, the customer GTS model was only available in Guards Red and left-hand drive. Customer GTR models were painted white only. Both models could be identified by the transparent fairings over the (non pop-up) headlamps and more aggressively flared bodywork compared to the standard GT.

CHAPTER 2
THE 944-DYNAMITE !

A NEW GENERATION

This chapter's explosive title was the enthusiastic reaction of *Porsche Panorama* (magazine of the Porsche Club of America) to their first experience with the Porsche 944 in April 1982.

The new car was first seen officially in September 1981, but its coming did not catch many Porsche watchers by surprise. On a visit to Weissach with the British Porsche Club in May that year, I and several others managed a close look at a development engine fitted to a 924 in one of the test shops. Anyone who went to Le Mans the same year also realised that the 2.5-litre engine in the 924 Carrera GTP did not owe much of its ancestry to Audi. Of course, the new car was very eagerly awaited; this was the next chapter in the development of the front-engine Porsche.

The 924 had been progressively developed beyond its original low-cost concept. Owners had continued to ask for improvements, not just with the engine but in the already good handling and the styling. The reality of marketing life, especially in the USA, was that customers were finding the 924 a fine example of the marque in terms of handling and looks, but that the engine was weak and noisy and the ride poor. Drivers were turning to the better-value products from Mazda and Datsun. In

Europe, the situation was not much better, with price differentials from country to country drawing criticism from many long-time Porsche enthusiasts. In its own backyard though, Porsche sales were still good. The company had accepted at an early stage of the 924's life that they should build their own engines to break the dependence on Audi for power units. Supplying their own engine would not only be more profitable, but combined with many other detail improvements, should finally convince the doubters that this new model was a Porsche in every sense of the word.

The 944 used the 924 Turbo rolling body/chassis, with visible aerodynamic changes that gave the new car a productionised 924 Carrera GT look. The bulged lines of the 944 were softer than the GT and the new panels were all in zinc-coated steel. The flexible polyurethane used for the wings of the GT (and the lower volume front and rear sections of the 928) were considered too high a technical risk as a process for the volumes expected with the 944.

The 944's looks really took the 924's classical styling to a new level. There was no doubt that the flares did for the four-cylinder range what they had done for the 911 on the Turbo. The aggressive styling gave the 944 real presence and a head-turning

capability that the original 924 never enjoyed. It was soon given the Fuchs-style five-spoke alloy wheels so popular on the 911 (although not interchangeable), and a larger rear spoiler than the 924 Turbo. The front spoiler, combined with detail changes to the front bumper, gave the new model a completely different front aspect. In some respects there was so much colour-coded bodywork visible, you could be forgiven for thinking the car looked like an unfinished plastic kit!

Inside the car was straight 924 faults-and-all. The 924 cockpit was always totally functional if not loud in a fashion sense. The layout was proven and comfortable, with little more to be said. It took several more years before the dash was redesigned to eliminate the instrument visibility and ventilation grumbles that owners had with the original.

Top right: *This launch photo of the 944 shows off its aggressive styling.*

Bottom right: *Another launch shot revealing the strongly flared fenders and the larger rear spoiler.*

Above: *The front air dam came from the Carrera GT.*

Above right: *The flares 'productionised' the look started by the Carrera GT.*

The new engine fitted snugly into the 924 engine compartment.

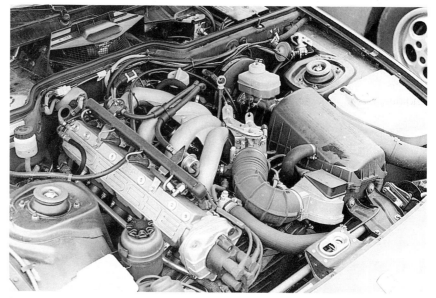

The brakes and suspension from the 924 Turbo were fitted and the choice was given of five-speed manual or three-speed automatic. The dog-leg first gear of the 924 Turbo was dead at last, with fifth gear to the top right from the standard 'H' pattern.

The new engine was designed so that it would fit the engine compartment of the 924. It had to be fuel efficient and meet worldwide emissions standards. But why choose a four? In a market where a six would have been considered a virtually automatic choice, to choose a difficult-to-balance large-capacity four takes some explaining, especially when the 924 engine was being criticised for its harshness.

For fuel efficiency and size – *also* the engine had to be fitted from below the car on the production line at Neckarsulm – the four came out best from the engineers' analysis. The development of the aluminium V8 in the 928, and the associated Thermally Optimised Porsche (TOP) cylinder head programme, had given them a detailed basis for the new engine's cylinder head design. The head was designed for commonality with the 928, with a single overhead camshaft operating two valves per

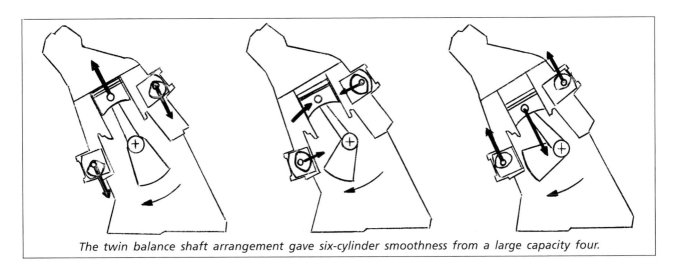

The twin balance shaft arrangement gave six-cylinder smoothness from a large capacity four.

cylinder through hydraulic tappets.

After extensive study, the problem of balance was solved by applying the separate balance shaft principle originally espoused by Lanchester, but using a two bearing arrangement patented by Mitsubishi of Japan.

Explained briefly, the problem that had to be solved by the Weissach engineers was not simply that of balancing the major oscillating and rotating components. Such balancing is important and will eliminate the primary free forces and moments. With an in-line four-cylinder engine, there will still be a vibrational source from the up and down movement of the piston and connecting rod masses, giving unbalanced secondary inertia forces. The Lanchester principle overcomes these secondary forces by the use of two counter rotating parallel shafts, running at twice crankshaft speed. The shafts have calculated imbalance and compensate the secondary imbalance of the pistons and rods. Such an arrangement gives the four-cylinder engine significantly improved overall smoothness, similar to that found naturally with an in-line six-cylinder engine.

The new engine used the Bosch Digital Engine Electronics (or Motronic) integrated injection and ignition control system seen for the first time on the Carrera GT and the 1981 924 Turbo. Whereas the 924 models used the K-Jetronic system, the new car used the L-Jetronic version.

The result was an engine which delivered good performance with notable smoothness, yet returned very good fuel efficiency and low emissions. Remarkably, the new engine weighed the same as the standard 924 Audi-derived unit. It had 30 per cent more power (160 bhp DIN/153 bhp SAE in European form, 150 bhp DIN/143 bhp SAE in USA form) and capacity went from 1984 cc to 2479 cc.

The designers went to considerable lengths to ensure isolation of the engine and transmission from the bodyshell. The engine was suspended on two engine mounting units. These were filled with anti-freeze and behaved like a shock absorber. Conventional rubber mounts were used for the rear mounted gearbox. The engine mountings have since come to give problems, but more of that later. The steering also came in for isolation treatment, the rack being suspended by rubber mountings from the crossmember upon which it was mounted.

The 1982 model 944 was received ecstatically by the press, who even compared it to the then-current 911SC. This time the car went on sale in the USA within $1000 of its nearest competitors, the Datsun 280ZX Turbo and the Alfa GTV 6/2.5. The 944 had a top speed of 132 mph and reached 60 mph in 8.3 seconds. In the USA, it replaced the 924 and 924 Turbo completely in the showrooms, which said it all about the official view of the comparison between the 924 and the 944.

Some said the 944 was what the 924 should have been in the first place, but as we know, that was not possible. The new car was an entirely evolutionary step for the 924 and it was a strong statement about the concept of the Porsche for the eighties. In the UK the new model was known as the 944 Lux.

944 DEVELOPMENTS

The 1983 model 944 was essentially unchanged from the launch model, simply because the main effort went into assembling the new car in sufficient quantities to meet the demand. There were, however, the usual new exterior colours and radio system improvements (a four-speaker system was available for the 944 from this model year). Among the options the 'cookie cutter' style wheels could be replaced by the traditional Porsche five-spoke forged alloy versions. Improvements for the 1984 model year were mainly cosmetic.

The start of production for the 1985 model year had been held up by the German metal workers' strike, but even so there was little new worth waiting for in the 944 area. Tinted glass was available with heated washer jets and of course, more colour changes. It was the customers that were prepared to wait until the Spring of 1985 that had their patience rewarded with a major technical upgrade.

The new oval dish was introduced to give tall drivers an easier time avoiding the steering wheel with their legs. Electric seat adjustment served to lift the smaller driver to an acceptable height. The new dash considerably improved the heating and ventilation at face level, although

it still seemed to be (traditionally!) difficult to control the output of the heating system. Other improvements included a fuel tank capacity increase from 66 to 80 litres and the fitting of tinted glass. These mods coincided with the 944 Turbo launch, and the 944 received the new car's (stiffer) cast alloy front suspension arms, replacing the old VW Golf (Rabbit) items dating back to the 924 era. Nineteen eighty-five saw the produc-

Mid-way through the 1985 model year saw the first major improvements to the 944, including an 'oval' dash layout.

tion total of the 944 pass 50,000 units since the launch in January 1982. In that time, its price in the UK had risen from approximately £14,000 to £21,673 in December 1986. This was the period when cynics said that the sum of Porsche development on the 944 was the annual board meeting to decide how much the company could put the price up without losing market share. That's perhaps a little hard, but the signs were there that the company was taking the success of their most important model for granted. There seemed to be more emphasis on getting maximum production volume, rather than consolidating the car's technical superiority or exclusiveness.

A 1988 944 shows off its 'telephone dial' wheels.

That so many customers perceived the slowing of the standard 944's development cycle would cost the business dearly in 1987. In the UK the passenger door mirror only became a standard item from 1985 and ABS (anti-lock braking) was only introduced as an option in 1987, well behind the rest of the industry.

In 1988, with total 944 production over 100,000, a general slump in demand hit Porsche very hard. There were significant cutbacks in production and rapid introduction of revised models into the market place to revitalise sales. For the 944, this meant an increase in capacity to 2.7 litres for the 1989 model year.

Performance was slightly better, especially the mid-range torque, but the customers clearly did not see enough in the car to stem the 944's decline. Sales continued to ebb, nowhere more so than in the crucial US market that the company had become so dependent on. In June 1989 further rationalisation of the product range resulted in the announcement that production of the 944 had ceased 'in readiness for the move of all four-cylinder production to Zuffenhausen'. It marked the end for the single camshaft, normally breathing engine and also confirmed the end of thinking that the company should provide an entry-level model in its range.

With such a short production life, the 2.7-litre 944 must become a good buy for the enthusiast in years to come. It won't attract the investor mentality car buyer, but will be special enough to maintain a good resale price.

944 TURBO

If the 944 was good the 944 Turbo was very good! With so much experience of turbocharging within Weissach, the blown version was completely predictable. The 924 Carrera GTP that had run at Le Mans in 1981 not only used the new 2.5-litre engine, but also a sixteen valve head and turbocharging. The fact that it took four more years to develop a production Turbo, albeit in eight valve form, gives some indication of the work that went into giving the new model total reliability, good low speed torque and still maintain the good emissions record. The car was launched in the Spring of 1985 (with

right-hand drive versions available in the UK from November that year). The power rating in all markets was the same, whether fitted with catalytic converter or not and it was designed to run on lead-free fuel. With 220 bhp and 239 lb ft peak torque at only 3500 rpm the car combined excellent handling with a 153 mph capability and a time to 62 mph of 6.3 seconds.

By comparison, the 911 Carrera of the same year gave 231 bhp from its 3.2 litres and only managed 203 lb ft torque at 4800 rpm. The time to 62 mph was a mere 0.2 seconds faster than the 944 Turbo, with the same maximum speed. *Car* magazine in the UK found that the front-

engined car returned better fuel consumption (30.6 mpg against 28.8 mpg and they commented that the 911's consumption dropped quickly below 20 mpg when it was driven hard. The 911 did have the edge in some areas, like superior traction (not surprisingly with the rearward weight bias) and driving position. Very importantly, the build quality of the Zuffenhausen-assembled 911 was seen as superior to the 944 Turbo and, of course, no

This 1988 944 Turbo shows off its rear underbody spoiler and machined finish wheels.

Porsche fan would dispute that the 911 sound would rival Glenn Miller for musical quality!

The consensus, however, was that the 944 Turbo was the better car, offering effortless driving pleasure and near-perfect road manners. The driver did not have to rev the engine to keep in the torque band and town driving was far less demanding. The practicality of the 944T may be a mundane additional benefit, but it all added up to the fact that the car was now a serious competitor to the 911 at an equal price.

Wider wheels and the logo identify the Turbo.

In the car, the engine of the Turbo looks much the same as that of the standard 944.

The 944 Turbo featured many improvements over the 944 and the 924 Turbo. On a technical level, there was considerable development to be seen in the area of the turbocharger, with a water-cooled bearing housing for the K26 KKK unit. One of the serious long-term reliability problems with the 924 Turbo had been the relatively short life of the Turbo. The enthusiast could stretch its life by careful handling (see Chapter 5) but such sensitive techniques were not acceptable for general customer usage with the new model. Without supplementary turbo cooling, temperature hot spots could break down the structure of a conventional multigrade oil (especially after engine shutdown) and cause extreme wear in the bearings and seals which support the impeller rotor. The 944 turbocharger's water-cooling system runs on after engine shutdown, until the oil in the housing falls below a pre-set maximum operating temperature. This prevents the oil's structure breaking down and, as a result, not protecting the bearings and seals on restart.

Another new feature was electronic boost pressure control, which replaced the previous method (a mechanical wastegate). The mechanical system was not considered to give satisfactory fuel consumption, especially at partial throttle. The turbocharging hardware was completed with an air-to-air intercooler, which reduced inlet temperature by 43°C (135°F), so significantly improving combustion efficiency and power output.

The heart of the engine was the Bosch Motronic engine management system. With total control of the injection, ignition and turbo boost this system also now included knock regulation.

Engine knocking is uncontrolled detonation of the fuel/air mixture. The condition can reveal itself if the timing is amiss or incorrect fuel is being used. It sounds like dried peas rattling in a tin can and if prolonged is damaging to the engine.

On the 944 Turbo a knock sensor was located between cylinders two and three. It picked up the harmful vibrations that were the result of knocking and the sensor's output was used by the Motronic processor to retard the timing until the knocking ceased (in a matter of milliseconds). This kept the ignition advance at the optimum efficiency for any given loading. Such sophistication also meant the engine could run on leaded or unleaded fuel. The Motronic unit merely retarded the ignition for any given loading to prevent knocking with the unleaded type.

The cylinder head design also broke new ground by the use of ceramic inserts cast into the exhaust ports. This gave better throttle response on acceleration and better catalytic conversion, both because the energy level in the exhaust gas flow was higher. An added bonus of this was that the engine cooling requirement was reduced. The higher performance from the blown engine also resulted in many basic strengthening modifications to the original 944 engine, for example, thicker cylinder liners and forged connecting

Top: *The skeleton of the 944 Turbo shows its 924 ancestry and the considerable development since the first cars. Note the cast suspension arms.*

Above: *Evolution! In front is a 944 Turbo, behind it is a 924 and then a 944. Below the bumper line, the front has changed considerably.*

Above left: *The dash of a Turbo. The boost gauge can just be seen at the base of the rev counter.*

rods. As is typical of the marque, every detail of the engine was analysed to assess acceptability for turbocharging and it meant the result was a significantly developed engine. The turbo was certainly no bolt-on goodie, it was a fourth generation concept that followed the path of the twin-turbo 1100 bhp Can-Am 917/30 of 1973, the 911 Turbo series from 1974 and the 924 Turbo programme from 1978. It was a confident demonstration of market-leading turbo technology.

It was not just the engine which received the attention of the engineers. The clutch was stronger and the five-speed gearbox was fitted with a separate oil cooler and stronger gears and bearings. Stopping power was considerable, prompting the PCA's *Porsche Panorama* magazine to comment that the brakes were strong enough to clean the bugs off the windshield! The front and rear ventilated disc brakes used four-piston aluminium calipers with forced air cooling.

The designers had worked hard on detail improvements to the basic 944 shape. At the front, the driving lights were integrated into a new flexible polyurethane spoiler, eliminating the separate bumper. At last the windshield was flush-fitted, and a skirt was added at the rear. The 'telephone dial' wheels from the 928 had

somehow found their way onto the new car also, but these didn't do the car's looks any favours.

The interior was updated with the new oval 944 dash, which regrouped the instruments, improved the heating and ventilation and gave a better driving position for taller drivers. The seats had electric position control to allow shorter drivers to raise the seat, if necessary.

The next road car development for the 944 Turbo was the Turbo S (known in the UK as 944 Turbo with Special Equipment), launched in the Spring of 1988. The idea was not new, because the late Al Holbert (then the US Porsche motorsports chief) had homologated a 944 Turbo 'S' for the SCCA SS class back in 1986 to take on the mighty Corvettes. In truth, these 1986 'S' Turbos were stripped out, blueprinted racers,

A 1989 250 bhp 944 Turbo, one of the outstanding sports cars of the eighties.

but they contributed much information to the roadgoing Turbo S of 1988. In Europe, more experience came from the one-make series for the 944 Turbo, known as the Turbo Cup. These were not so modified and even raced with catalytic converters. This didn't stop the racing being as exciting as any Formula Ford thrash though! Power for the new road car was 250 bhp, available only with catalytic converter fitted. This placed the Turbo S between the 911 Carrera and the 911 Turbo, with a top speed of 163 mph and a time of 5.7 seconds to 62 mph. The five-speed transmission was strengthened and a limited slip differential now became standard.

The 1990 model Turbo shows its 928-style split rear spoiler.

The 250 bhp model became the only turbocharged model available in August of 1989 and by then the much more appropriate 'machined'-finish forged alloy wheels were fitted. The looks were further enhanced for the 1990 year by the 928-style wing rear spoiler. The 944 Turbo remains an outstanding demonstration of Porsche's ability to design the ultimate practical sports car.

944S

Only Porsche could look at the 944 model range in 1985 and say, 'We have the 150 bhp 944 and the 220 bhp 944 Turbo so we will fill the gap with the 190 bhp 944S!'

The sixteen-valve 944S, launched in 1986, took further the cylinder head technology that had been proven at Le Mans in 1981 and developed on the road with the 928S4. The catalytic converter engine policy, adopted from the 944 Turbo, was carried over

The underplayed rear view of the 944S.

to the 'S'. The 944 engine was developed to take the sixteen-valve head and this meant new camshaft drive, intake and exhaust systems. The engine package was completed by the Bosch digital engine electronics system, but this latest version used two knock sensors.

Using four valves per cylinder also meant the same power rating could be offered with or without the catalytic converter fitted. The four-valve technology was used just as much to improve cylinder head breathing (and hence emissions) as it was to allow greater maximum rpm and power output. The exhaust camshaft was positioned where the previous single camshaft of the eight-valve 944 was found and it was driven from the crankshaft by a stronger, wider toothed belt. The intake camshaft was driven by a central chain (with a hydraulic tensioner) from the exhaust camshaft.

The cam lobes operated the valves directly through hydraulic cup tappets. The parallel valve arrangement allowed the spark plugs to be located centrally in the crossflow combustion chamber, giving good mixture burn characteristics and, as a result, low exhaust emissions. The four-valve head gave the 944 not only improved power, but also greater torque, espe-

The 944S engine shows off its twin camshaft, four valves per cylinder technology.

The '16 Ventiler' logos were optional.

cially in the mid and upper rev ranges. The engine was rev-limited (by fuel cut-off) to 6800 rpm, against the two-valve 944 maximum of 6500 rpm. This meant a top speed of 143 mph and a time to 62 mph of 7.9 seconds.

Outside the engine compartment, the 'S' shared ABS as a new option with the other 1986 944 models. Why this important safety feature was not standard on a car that took so much care not to pollute the environment is unclear. It is unfortunate indeed that the rapid developments in anti-lock braking systems seem to have caught Porsche unawares and they were slow into the marketplace compared with other (especially European) manufacturers.

The gearbox was the same as used on the Turbo, but with adjusted ratios. The fuel consumption was outstanding for a car in this class with an average 33 mpg possible. The suspension was 944 Turbo with the stiffer cast alloy front suspension arms, which also were fitted to the 1986 model 944 for commonality of parts.

Outwardly, the 944S looked virtually identical to the standard 944. One could specify a '16-valve' logo on the sides ahead of the doors, but otherwise the only difference was the 'S' after the '944' near the tailgate. Inside the engine compartment, the magnesium cam cover, with its centrally located spark plugs, easily set it apart from the standard 944.

The press reaction to the 944S was measured. It was predictable that a twin cam engine would produce its power at higher revs than a more flexible single cam unit. The 944S must be worked to get the best from the engine, with maximum torque at 4300 rpm, against the standard car's maximum at 3000 rpm. The extra 40 bhp could be found easily enough on the open road, but it did not offer the performance margin over the standard 944 that might have been expected from the extra eight valves.

944S2

The 'S' performance problem was readily solved by the second series, introduced for the 1989 model year. It was a natural evolution with the engine keeping the sixteen-valve head, but with capacity enlarged to 3 litres. The engineers maintained interchangeability with the heads on the 928S4 and an extra 21 bhp came not only from the extra swept volume, but also changes to many details like valve springing.

The 3-litre block was all-new, featuring cooling technology from the TAG F1 programme. As well as increased stiffness from siamesed cylinders, the coolant volume in the block was reduced from 1.1 litres to 0.55 litres. This was possible following development that showed almost no cylinder cooling was required below combustion chamber level. The F1 knowledge resulted in lower oil capacity and less power loss from oil 'foaming'. The engine used tighter toleranced components and a plastic sump moulding. As an aside, it remains to be seen whether the increased use of plastics on cars will be environmentally acceptable in the long term (owing to the disposal problem).

Now fitted with Turbo bodywork the new 'S2' achieved a top speed of 150 mph with a time to 62 mph of 7.1 seconds, a significant improvement over the older car.

The S2 became the cheapest Porsche from the start of the 1990 model year with the discontinuation of the 2.7-litre 944.

First seen at the 1985 Frankfurt Motor Show, the 944 Cabriolet was a design study aimed at sensing public opinion to the idea. Reaction was very positive and the result was an agreement with the American Sunroof Corporation, who have built a brand new factory in Heilbronn, West Germany. 944 coupé bodyshells are converted by Porsche and considerably strengthened. They are clothed by ASC to form what must be the most elegant of all Porsche's 'rag tops'. The lines of the Cabriolet with the top closed have an almost Italian feel, but clearly capture the old 356 Speedster character from the rear three-quarter. As standard, the roof is operated electrically so that the roof can be closed from the driver's seat. The car will still seat four, but the rear luggage area has

Only the logo on the back marks the outward difference between this 3-litre 944S2 and the Turbo.

This pre-launch photo of the Cabriolet only gives a hint of this the most elegant of Porsche's 'rag tops'.

been reduced to allow space to stow the roof. The new car was launched in the Spring of 1989 with sixteen-valve 944S2 specification. The price reflected the company's push up-market. Its resultant exclusivity plus open good looks guarantee it to be a future classic.

THE FUTURE
Probably the most difficult period in Porsche's history as a car manufacturer were the years 1987/88. In the US sales dipped dramatically, due in part to the prevailing weakness of the dollar against the main European currencies. This forced US showroom prices to rise for little perceived improvement in value. With Japanese competition so strong, it was not surprising sales were hit badly, with

production volumes dropping by over 30 per cent in 1988 compared to 1987. By 1989, sales were still faltering and the 944 was discontinued, ostensibly in preparation for the move of four-cylinder production to Zuffenhausen. The company was attracting the attention of hostile predators by this time (such as Daimler-Benz, Audi-VW and Ford) who were casting envious eyes on Porsche's assets, particularly the Engineering Centre at Weissach. The medicine prescribed by Chief Executive Officer Heinz Branitzki and his team was higher working efficiency and more product exclusivity. By January 1990 it appeared to be working, the company declaring that its profits in the year to July 1989 were comfortably back in the black. Surely this was good news for the company's friends the world over. As Porsche moved on to a new chapter in its continuing history, there was comfort in the knowledge that the business still had

the reserves necessary to develop new products. Porsche's new strength in 1989 was summed up by the successive launches of the Carrera 4, 2, 944 Cabrio and 928GT. These were not the actions of a weakened company.

The next question we ask is where will the 944 go from 1990?

Retiring Research and Development Director Helmutt Bott has gone on record as saying that there is a 3.3-litre engine in development. It is also easy to speculate that there will be a sixteen-valve 3-litre Turbo available soon. It seems surprising that the sixteen-valve engine has not been turbocharged before, especially when that 924 Carrera GTP had it all back in 1981. The answer probably lies in the level of emissions from such an engine and the simple fact that not everything can be done at once.

Porsche have always championed the environmental compatibility of their cars and this is likely to remain

The short-lived 2.7-litre 944 looked much the same from the outside as previous models.

a major area of development. Already the cars are asbestos free (from 1988) and all have charcoal filters in the fuel tank venting to prevent vapour escape. All, of course, run on lead-free fuel and most markets now demand the inclusion of catalytic converters. Future effort is likely to include the increased use of environmentally friendly materials and improved engine efficiency with reduced noise.

Fuzzy photographs have been published of a totally restyled 944 for 1991, looking more rounded and clearly evolved from the 928S4, with integrated rear lighting and flexible rear bodywork. In the transmission field, the successfully raced PDK automatic gearbox has been evaluated in a 944 and has been launched as the Tiptronic option in the 911 Carrera 2 in 1990. If the costing is right, it must eventually be offered in the same way for the four-cylinder cars.

In spite of the business pressure, the Porsche ethic that it should offer an affordable entry-level model may still survive. There has been some information that Weissach has been studying a new entry-level sports car. This has been code numbered 984 and could be a four-cylinder mid-engined two-seater of about 2 litres. Even the most optimistic must currently regard the future of this project with some doubt.

As in all 'jungle' situations, however, it is the fittest that survive and the 1990 four-cylinder models are outstanding sports cars with real performance and practical appeal across a wide market.

The emphasis is not now to produce as many cars as possible (very unpopular with the company's regular customers) but to consolidate the up-market position with technologically advanced sports cars.

CHAPTER 3

BUYING

INTRODUCTION

New Porsches have a reputation for performance, superior quality of build (including in corrosion resistance) and reliability. Used models go one better, since they also have a reputation for low depreciation rates. The 924 and 944 are not as good an investment as an older 911 – yet – but still far better than most other makes, especially the Italian and Japanese sports cars that claim to compete with them in the marketplace. The low depreciation rate comes also from the exclusivity given by the relatively low build numbers.

The accountant's eyes really light up when the limited edition models enter the discussion. The best 924/944 investments come from the Carrera GT series, which with time will compete with the 911 Carrera RS for exclusivity. More modest budgets can be used on the cosmetic limited editions, where special trim and exterior colour schemes have been offered. These models are not in the 'classic' category of collectable Porsches, but should hold their own against serious depreciation in the long term.

The most important aspect of buying a Porsche is to understand what is on offer, knowing the standard features and what are options.

PART 1

GENERAL
INFORMATION

What this chapter sets out to do is inform, to show what to look for and where, but it is down to your experience to make the selection. These words cannot make the decision for you. I'm the first person to admit that there will be cars for sale that have oddities or problems that are unique and not mentioned here. If a car needs work, don't politely ignore it. If you think it is within your capabilities to fix it and you still want the car, work out how much it would cost to fix professionally and make the seller an offer. Use your know-

When buying, look past the name on the bonnet, the seductive styling and the wide wheels and coldly consider the value for money.

ledge to bring down the prices! If you don't think you have the inclination, capability or the resources to have the car fixed, just leave it, there will be others! The cost of unforeseen repairs to Porsches is legendary. Such bills can ruin your first Porsche experience, and that would indeed be a distortion of 'driving in its purest form'.

The decision about which model you will be seeking will be determined by the obvious factor: money. Compared to the 911, both the 924 and 944 offer a more recent model

An expensive option a Porsche cellphone fitted to the centre tunnel of this 944.

for the same cash.

Used car buyers always tend to think of the base model as the norm when it comes to a price guide. If your car has a lot of expensive factory options, the car may not make the price the seller expects. For the

four-cylinder range, this applies especially to key options like the passenger door mirror, radio and on early cars, electric windows and rear wiper. These essential accessories tend to make the car only more desirable rather than increasing its value. Proof of certain special options like the Club Sport package would add a premium to the price, but be convinced the car was fitted like this from new.

COST OF OWNERSHIP
Best value in any Porsche is the model that is more than three years old but less than seven. This is because the initial rapid depreciation stage has been passed and yet the Longlife guarantee is still in place on the bodyshell. The design technology applied to the cars is now such that a well-serviced seven-year-old can be in virtually showroom condition, with no serious concern areas. These cars also can have a reasonable total mileage and with careful ownership, will be unlikely to need major engine/transmission work. It is important that there is evidence of proper regular servicing (which also verifies the distance reading). If it's relevant, you should check the annual bodywork inspections have been performed, to preserve the Longlife guarantee. Because the corrosion protection was so effective, the real bar-

A well-serviced older car can be in virtually showroom condition. This 1979 model is getting a free engine diagnosis at the 1984 Silverstone 1000 Km meeting.

gains can be found in the cars over five years old. I'm assuming here that your roads are not blanketed in salt from the end of Autumn to the beginning of Summer. In that type of environment very special care will have been required to keep even a Porsche looking fresh. Generally, the older models may require a little more care and attention, but a looked-after example will be inexpensive to buy and run.

Spares for the 924 or the 944 are not a problem. Through its dealers, the factory provides a high level of parts support for the older models. The older established dealers do provide many of the more regularly used parts over the counter. The cost of genuine factory parts is not cheap, which can partly be justified by low volumes and the performance application. Non-factory parts are univer-

sally condemned, because of the unknown safety implications. That said, the 924 was manufactured using many VW/Audi parts, that will fit straight off the VW store shelf. It is always worth checking to see if the part that is needed is a VW (especially Golf/Rabbit) item, as the cost will be less.

Aside from the Official Porsche Centres and certain well-known specialists, servicing can be a problem

Above: *Know what you are buying. This is the chassis plate for an XJ specification 924 (see appendices).*

Top: *The chassis numbers for later 924 and all 944 models will be found on the right-hand firewall in the engine compartment.*

as quality varies enormously. There are many who have set themselves up as Porsche specialists, who have no proper training, experience or equipment. The safest way of finding a good servicing shop is to talk to local Porsche Club members. Failing that, study the Club magazines and go and look at a prospective workshop. Talk to the owner and look at the other cars in the shop. If there are no Porsches, be wary! If yours is

enthusiasts will want to do most of the work themselves, for cost reasons. The hourly rate for a reputable specialist restorer is also very high. The best way to balance cost and get a professional job done is to learn the time consuming jobs and contract out the high-skill work or those requiring expensive tools. It depends on how much satisfaction is gained from such a job, which will invariably take much longer and require

In the UK, the 924 and 944 generally fall into group 8, with the 924 Turbo, 944 Turbo and 944S edging into Group 9. This compares with Group 6 for a VW Golf (Rabbit) GTi or Group 7 for a BMW 325i.

HOMEWORK
The first step for the used Porsche purchaser is to do some homework. Before buying, take a long look at the publications listed below. Get the

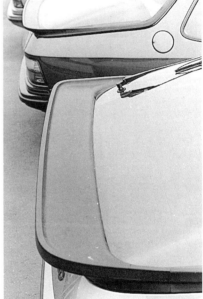

Most enthusiasts will want to do most of the work themselves. This is PCGB member Cliff Judd's pristine 1979 924.

more effort than originally thought. It also depends on whether one has a need to use the car in the meantime.

INSURANCE
It pays to shop around for insurance. Talk to the brokers that advertise in the Club magazines as they can very often provide more competitive quotes than local brokers. If the car is a cherished model or limited edition then a special insurance will be required that agrees its market value with then insurer.

Rear spoiler differences, the nearest one is larger and is fitted to the 944 range. The smaller type at the rear was the 924 style.

feel for the market and what can be bought with the money available. Do this for at least four weeks before attempting to purchase anything. Remember that most sellers will discount against their asking price, if presented with a bank draft or cash. It's crude, but it works, especially if there has not been too much demand for the car. This means that when the homework stage is being

an older model, be sure that they know what they are doing. This latter even applies to the newer Official Centres, who may not have much experience of the older models. The main problem with servicing is the labour rate. The Official Centres (rightly) set themselves up as the best, but they are very expensive.

Professional restoration is now quite an industry, but many

done, adverts with asking prices up to 5-10 per cent more than the money available can be considered, but be realistic. The Official Centres are probably the most expensive places to buy a used Porsche, but they do carry virtually new-car guarantees for quality and reliability. Again, the homework will identify how much this extra peace of mind will cost. Buying privately will carry more risk, but be cheaper. Private deal prices will be approximately midway between the trade and showroom retail price for the year. Be very wary of suspect cars when buying from a non-specialist trader or privately.

The magazines and newspapers that carry sports car classified advertising will probably be well known to the reader. Guidelines as to prices and availability can be gained from monthly magazines and certain newspapers.

In the UK, the magazines suggested by the author might be (in no particular order) *Classic Cars*, *Classic & Sports Car* and *Motor Sport*. The car buying market is a national one in Britain and the *Exchange & Mart* and the *Sunday Times* are the two best sources of Porsches every week. The *Sunday Times* is the main source for the more recent used models, whether buying from the trade or privately. *Porsche Post* is the journal of the Porsche Club Great Britain and adverts (both trade and private) appear in every issue. Attending local regional pub nights, held in most areas every month, can also be an invaluable source of non-advertised cars.

In the USA, the world's biggest Porsche Club, the PCA, publish the excellent *Porsche Panorama* monthly. This carries pages of adverts (again both trade and private) but because of the geographical size of the country, it may not be so practical to buy, unless the seller is close. The Club is organised into regions and most of these have their own newsletters, which can be a more practical source. Aside from local dealers and regional newspaper classified ads, other more national sources are *Road & Track* magazine and *Hemmings Motor News*. It all depends on how much travelling you want to do.

P A R T 2
SELECTION

924 MODELS TO 1985

The 2-litre 924 models are currently the Porsche bargains. They offer the opportunity to own a good condition Porsche for a relatively low outlay. Considering that all 924 types to 1980 had galvanised underbodies, a well looked after example can main-

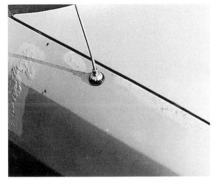

tain a sound body structure and be completely reliable. Those models after 1980 were even better value, since the whole bodyshell was fully galvanised and there was a seven year anti-rust-perforation guarantee on the bodyshell. In the UK, nearly all the cars imported were to the higher Lux specification.Each new 924 model year up to 1982 produced new refinement (see Appendix 1) but this also lifted list prices well beyond the original entry-level idea. After 1982 the technical improvement virtually ceased, until the big change to the 2.5-litre engine

Left: *This is corrosion caused by build-up of debris in the wheel arches and penetration of the underbody sealing. The wing should be replaced.*

Above: *A bad case of corrosion to the front spoiler of a 1977 model 924. Note the seam has been filled, a warning sign that serious corrosion is underneath.*

in 1986. You will get a better car stretching the budget to afford say a 1981, rather than a 1980 model, but after that, the benefit will be largely one of lower mileage.

Mechanically, the main things to look out for are high mileage engines (noisy and smokey) with worn-out valve guides and seats and worn bearings in the torque shaft. The later '911 pattern' five-speed versions offer a better transmission option, but most cars to 1979 will have the original four-speed layout. The engine runs fairly hot with oil pressure at idle as low as 1bar/15psi on an engine ready for overhaul. 2bar/30psi is about right for a low mileage engine.

The electrical system appears complicated, with lots of relays, but is reasonably straightforward. The

PORSCHE 924

heater fan is always idling, which is annoying and it is a design oversight that there seems to be no way to stop heat from coming out of the centre outlets, whatever the control position. If the body looks OK, then what you see is generally what you will get.

The 924 suffered very badly with poor hot starting until steps were taken in 1980/1 to overcome fuel vapour lock and drainage from the fuel metering unit after shutdown. The earlier cars can, however, be modified and this is covered in the Chapter 6.

924 TURBO

The Cinderella of the 924 range, which promised so much and for some reason did not sell as it should. The 924 Turbo came in two series. The S1 was the (European) 170 bhp version, manufactured from 1979 to the start of the 1981 model year. The S2 version was made for 1981 and 1982 and was the 177 bhp version. The later type is the one that is the most desirable, because of the increased power, digital engine elec-

The 170 bhp Series One 924 Turbo.

tronics and consequently better fuel consumption. 924 Turbos generally have a poor reputation for burning out turbos. The later series are better than the earlier ones, because they have better crankcase breathing to maintain oil circulation after shutdown. When buying any 924 Turbo, a genuine mileage is an important factor, because on average, the turbo

has been found to last about 40,000 miles, before replacement is necessary. It's not all bad because a well looked after turbo can be trouble-free and last longer than the average, but when you are buying you need proof of careful ownership and ideally documentary evidence of the mileage and age of the turbo.

I would rate the 924S2 Turbo amongst the best of any of the production Porsche models manufactured to 1982, including the 911. With all buying precautions taken and a sound car purchased, it will prove to be a thoroughly fast and practical car that has a progressively maturing classic status.

The 177 bhp Series Two model. The side repeaters are the visible external difference.

924 CARRERA GT

The most collectable of the 924 and 944 series to date. Included here would obviously be the GTS and GTR, if they are available. Be very sure that

48

what is for sale is an original, by checking the chassis and engine number against the factory lists (see Appendices). A secure history is everything for this type of car, so spend time checking this out with the organisations that have serviced the car and even previous owners.

Check very carefully for crash damage and that all panels are to the original specification. The Carrera GT falls into the investment category of cherished cars and, as such, identified mechanical problems should be weighed up against the selling price and the likely rate of rise in value in future years. This is not a car to buy without a fair amount of homework beforehand. On a detailed mechanical level, most of what was said for the 924 Turbo applies, especially relating to wear on the valve guides. The Carrera GT was only produced in three colours, namely black, silver and red.

944

The reliability of the 2.5-litre Porsches is generally very good especially up to 30,000 miles. There are several areas that the buyer should take into account especially when looking at older (pre 1984) 944s.

The item that makes experienced 944 owners most nervous is the unreliability of the early camshaft timing belt. It must be said that if the car has been properly serviced throughout its life this need not be a problem, as the service shop will know of the potential problem. Initially, expert opinion advised that the belt should be checked every 10 to 12,000 miles for tension and signs of damage or fraying, with replacement mandatory at 30,000 miles. SInce 1985 the factory have fitted the stronger 944 Turbo belt and if the car is properly serviced it should not be a further cause for concern. Retrofit-

Polyurethane front spoiler of the 944. This one has optional front driving lamps.

ting of the later belt is possible on the early cars, but it should be done by a specialist. An automatic tensioner was fitted from the 1987 models which has made life a lot easier for the mechanics, whose knuckles used to get a hard time setting the tension to the close tolerances required.

The consequences of not following the recommended advice has been, in some cases, total failure of the timing belt with resultant bent valves, damaged pistons and worse. It follows from the above that a consistent service history is a vital requirement when buying.

Another problem that has since been overcome concerned the fluid filled engine mountings. The fault was not so bad that the car could not be used, but the units could leak fluid, especially on the (hot) exhaust side of the engine. The symptom of a failed mounting would be rough

idling and the failure could be confirmed when evidence of the leakage could be seen around the mounting.

These faults have produced improved mountings and better heat protection from the factory. The latest mountings have an orange paint stripe around their base and can be retrofitted to any 944 model. Information on the hydraulic engine mountings can be found in Chapter 5. Amongst the less frequent major problems noted is head gasket failure, which can allow the oil and water to mix. For the 944, with its unlined aluminium bores this can lead to deeply marked bores and even a new block being required. Mixing of the oil and water has also happened following failure of the oil/water intercooler assembly (again, see Chapter 5). The only way to be sure that this will not happen on a used car is to take the cooler apart and check the matrix and its seals.

This is the extent of the predictable bad news. With a little tender loving care and attention all the negatives are avoidable. The 944 is a sound purchase for everyday use and will convert even a dedicated 911 driver to its practical yet rapid form of transport.

On a final note, don't forget the end-of-line 2.7-litre models. These will acquire some desirability with time, not only because of the larger engine, but because of the shortness of the production run.

944 TURBO/944S

As always with more recent models, look out for crash damage and a consistent service history. The general guidelines given in Part 3 should reveal any causes for concern with these models. Remember that the car may well not have been looked after and may even have been raced. For the UK buyer this is a comparatively recent subject to be concerned about when buying a Porsche. The easiest way to check on whether a car has a racing background is to lift the rear floor carpets and look for roll-over bar mounting points on the under-tray or the rear wheel arches.

The advice is stretch to a 944S2 rather than the early S, since the performance of the latter may disappoint. That said, the early 944S is

'If you've got it; flaunt it!'
Extravert decal on the 944 Turbo.

Late model complexity; four-pot caliper and ABS sensor (on the strut) on a 1989 944S2.

now a value-for-money Porsche, which the impecunious enthusiast should probably consider. The S2 Cabrio will become a much sought-after classic in years to come and its second-hand price will reflect this growing status.

From 1989 the Turbo was sold at the higher 'Turbo Cup' specification, first seen on the limited edition Turbo S in 1988. The prices between the 1988 and 1989 models reflect this difference.

P A R T   3

LOOKING

These are a few notes suggesting what to look for when viewing a prospective purchase. It is not a comprehensive guide and it is assumed that you have bought (successfully) second-hand cars previously. Consequently, you will know NEVER to buy a car at night, in the rain, under artificial light, without seeing the proof of ownership and so on (but we all have!).

Don't ignore the first impression of the car. Just walking up to it can give valuable information. Is the colour right? Does it look tatty? Is there something missing?

THE BODY
The first impression given by looking at a well-looked after body should be one of cleanliness, even down to the wheel wells and the door hinge areas. Stone chips should be touched-in and there will be evidence of wax-oil protection throughout the underbody.

1) Look for evidence of previous accidents. Look along the sides and roof of the car at eye level. Are there any paint or panel irregularities? Ripples or rough paint surface indicate a cheap repair, possibly covering filler (and rust). Are the door, engine lid and rear glass gaps symmetrical all round their openings? Is there evidence of repainting of certain panels or the entire car? It is very difficult to

An apparently clean 924 Carrera GT. Looking closer reveals that the car has been extensively dismantled. Note the irregular gaps around the headlamps and poorly fitted polyurethane wings. Be very wary when signs such as this are evident.

match metallic paint. Decide yourself whether this factor alone guides you to buy a car of solid colour, rather than a metallic one. Look for overspray on difficult-to-mask areas and items. These might be mouldings, trim strips, window surrounds and

Another view of the same car. Note the poorly fitted rear bumper and the overtightening of the polyurethane extensions, which has distorted the plastic.

PORSCHE 924

suspension parts. At the rear, look up to the number plate lights, as these often get missed when masking up for a quick respray.

Check the original paint code decal (behind the engine splashwall) is the same as the actual colour of the car.

Look under the car at the under-tray to see if it is distorted in any irregular way. Look for evidence that the underbody protection has been damaged and repaired, especially at the front. This will show as non-standard colour or unusually clean areas. Lift the carpets over the rear wheel wells, to check the car has not had a roll-over bar fitted at any stage of its life. Old racers should be put out to grass!

2) For the older cars, especially pre-1981 models where only the undertray, front and rear wings and sills were zinc-coated, rust attack must be considered. The key areas are shown in the diagram in Chap-

ter 4. Even a fully zinc-coated bodyshell will rust freely if an accident repair has been performed unsatisfactorily. Look for clean wheel arches with no debris build-up and clear drainage holes. Moisture

trapped in debris will attack the structure through pin-holes or cracks in the undersealing. Stone-chips can wreak havoc on the front of a car if they have been unattended.

Rotten front wings can be easily replaced, but the rear ones will need careful cutting and re-welding.

Look inside the rear luggage area and lift the carpets completely and take out the spare wheel. Look for debris and moisture build up in the two sidewells and the wheel well. Probe these to check for rust attack. At the bottom of each rear sidewell there is a little rubber seal. It should be free to move in the drain hole (to let water out).

As a final note, regard any customisation of the body as a non-contributor to the value of the car. In many cases customisation will make a car very difficult to sell.

On early 924 models, even well looked after examples will have needed some attention to stone chips to the front spoiler.

52

Looking down into a sidewell in the rear luggage compartment. Check the grommet at the base. Moisture here will cause internal condensation on the glass.

Above right: *Check the condition of the Space-saver wheel and the excellent Bilstein alloy lifter. Check also the tool kit is complete.*

ENGINE AND GEARBOX

If the engine is cold, start it and allow it to warm up. Consider the following:

1) Is the engine difficult to start from cold? Do the revs fluctuate when idling or miss when the throttle is pulsed? These suggest fuel or electrical systems may need specialist attention.

2) Is there excessive oil leakage from the engine, either from the camshaft cover gasket or underneath? Check the dipstick for the oil colour and whether water is present (blown head gasket?). Oil leakage from a 944 engine could mean a cheap

repair or poor servicing and result in high wear rates. Reject a 944 if there is evidence of engine oil leakage. Oil from the ends of the crankcase may indicate worn oil seals. The front oil seal on the 924 can be replaced fairly easily, with the engine in the car. The rear seal will need a stripdown.

Because of the difficulty of setting the timing belt tensions on the 944, any leakage from the front of the engine should be considered a specialist maintenance job.

3) Ask whether any major work has been done on the engine and check with crankcase visual inspection (fresh sealing compound, etc). Be impressed by a clean and tidy engine. It indicates regular attention. There should be no paint or heavy grease obscuring any part of the engine block (which might cover epoxy or welded repairs). Check the engine mountings on a 944 for the faults described earlier.

4) Check out the exhaust system. Look at both silencer boxes, or the catalytic converter, which will be fitted in place of the front box. Check the system is sound and not rusted out. Look for evidence of welding to fill rusted holes. The area where this can be seen most easily is the inner end of the chrome tailpipe sleeve.

Be impressed by a clean and tidy engine.

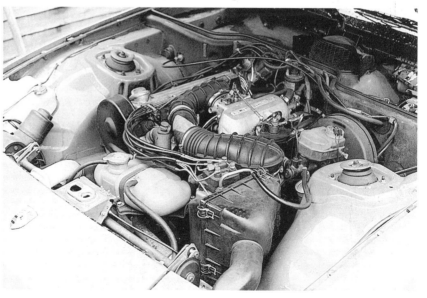

It may not look much now, but this corrosion to the plated parts inside the engine will quickly worsen and eventually could affect their function. This 1989 944 has probably been near salt water and will need a good underbody clean.

This is a good water trap and older tailpipes often split at the top at this point. On 924 Turbos, the manifolding around the turbo and to the front box is stainless steel. Because of the high temperature variations it experiences, cracking is possible around the flanges into the turbo. The pipe will show evidence of blowing past a crack. It can be welded using special equipment but for easy assembly, this should be done on a special jig.

Normally a 924/944 non-stainless system will be good for three to four years life, in a temperate climate. This will shorten if the roads are salted heavily in Winter.

5) Is the gearbox casing leaking or showing evidence of damage? Smal!

drips are not a problem but obvious heavy leakage suggests contact with the road surface. If the gearbox oil seals are found to be leaking, then accept that a rebuild is needed. See Chapter 8 for data on automatic gearboxes.

6) With the engine warm, rev the engine to about 3000 rpm in neutral. If a 924, does the engine sound like eggs frying in a pan? Check the exhaust for smoke as the engine is revved. This means worn valve guides (and a cylinder head stripdown) or worse, worn piston rings. If a 924 Turbo, the smoky exhaust can also mean a worn turbo, which will be very expensive to replace. Find out prices from a specialist before you agree a price for a car that needs this sort of work. If the owner says the turbo has been replaced ask to see the invoices.

Sit in the car and depress the clutch several times. The engagement should not be at the upper end of the movement, suggesting a worn clutch. Is the torque tube from the engine to the gearbox audible each time it is spun up (as the clutch is released)? A little noise as the shaft picks up is acceptable and will not need attention. Significant extra noise will mean a stripdown and torque tube replacement.

SUSPENSION, WHEELS AND TYRES

1) Clean, shiny wheels make a very good impression on any buyer, but check both sides of each wheel for any damage. Look also for worn or damaged tyres.
2) Inspect the shock absorbers for any signs of leakage and 'bounce' the body at each corner to check that they work satisfactorily (see Chapter 8).
3) Inspect the brake discs for signs of heavy grooving and if they have worn

a lip at their edges, replacement is necessary. If the brake pipes are heavily corroded and/or are leaking they must be replaced.
4) Check the lower control arms (especially the fabricated VW items) for damage. The damage may also be confirmed by uneven wear on a front tyre. Look also for play in the steering and splits in the steering rack gaiters.

INTERIOR AND TRIM

The ideal is an original, well kept interior, with sound and clean carpets.

opposite right: *The ideal is an original well-kept interior. Particularly impressive is the cleanliness and condition of the seats.*

1) Check the carpets for dampness. This could mean a leaking sunroof panel, windshield surround or blocked drainage behind the engine splash wall (leaking into the footwells). The rear luggage area carpet may be damp simply from spillage off the opening glass when it has been raining, but check the window sealing.
2) Check the spare wheel for use and damage and the inflation compressor (where fitted) for function. Check the car tools and lifting device are all present and working.
3) Examine the seats, including the seat backs, for damage and wear. Check the seat suspension is satisfactory. Beware a low mileage car with a well sagged driver's seat. It suggests the declared mileage may not be real. Check that seats function correctly, particularly where the driver's seat is electrically adjustable.
4) Check the headlining for tears or marks. A non-smoker's car is preferable, because there will be minimal discolouration of the fabric.

Above: *Check the fit of the sun-roof and inspect the carpets for signs of water leakage.*

Right: *Later models have a revised tailgate moulding which stops the rain water from dripping into the rear luggage area.*

Far right: *The sign of a loved car! Top condition tool kit and documentation.*

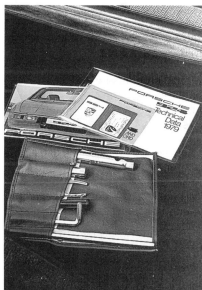

PORSCHE 924

Look for untidy wiring under the dash. Has that cellphone been wired in professionally?

5) Inspect the area under the dash. Is the wiring professionally tidy? Untidy wiring suggests previous problems with electrics. Check everything electrical works, especially the mirrors (check heating by touch) and windows.

ROAD TEST
You should always drive the car before making a decision to buy. Adequate insurance will be necessary for this and take care, especially if the weather is wet for your test.
1) The hot engine should start up easily, without excessive turning of

the engine. If a pre-1981 model 924, see Chapter 6 on vaporisation, otherwise diagnosis of fuel or electrical system is required.
2) A slipping clutch will reveal itself on pulling away and during driving as over-revving on acceleration or in cruise. A new clutch is required to remedy this.
3) Oil pressure should be 4-6 bar under load and depending on temperature. Pressure can drop to under 1 bar at hot idle.
4) Do all gears engage freely? Worn synchromesh will mean a gearbox rebuild.
5) Does the car steer in a straight line with hands off? Make allowances for road camber, especially if wide tyres are fitted. If the car steers continu-

ously off course, there is possible undetected crash damage to a suspension member or, worse still, a twisted chassis. The problem may only be a sticking brake pad, worn track rod end or a heavily marked disc. Is the problem amplified by braking? Have this problem checked by a specialist if you are unsure about the car. Otherwise assume the worst.
6) In normal driving are there any whines or vibrations from the transmission or wheel assemblies? It must be expected that older cars will have transmission whine to some extent. 944 models have been susceptible to front wheel vibrations, but later models have been improved by better suspension linkages. Tyres need to be balanced perfectly. Are there any

unexpected impact noises? Worn drive shaft couplings will give a 'thump, thump' noise from the rear axle.

7) Check the car has the same handling feel and response through left and right-hand bends. If the feel is different this may indicate past accident damage.

MAKING THE DECISION

Don't ignore those first impressions. The key factors are the history, the current condition and the cost to bring the car to the standard you want. Trade this off against the asking price, if there are no big problems. The car may already be priced to reflect a known problem. Consider also, that with further effort a better car, or a similar condition model at a lower price, could be found. If there is a big problem and unless the car is something special, don't buy it, there will be plenty of others!

It is a common factor across all well-looked after Porsches, young and

First impressions are important, but learn all you can about the car's history.

old, that they have excellent reliability to go with the performance. The buyer who carefully sorts the good from the bad will be very happy with the eventual purchase. Be patient in the search!

CHAPTER 4
BODYWORK

This chapter will be divided into three parts. The first will consider general care of the bodyshell and minor paintwork maintenance. The second part will consider some relevant detail maintenance and the final part will consider bodyshell customisation.

PART 1

GENERAL CARE

One of the comforting aspects about the 924/944 series is that the range has all featured part or fully zinc-coated steelwork. This means that the 'basket-case' 924 is virtually unheard of. The technology that enabled the initially six- and then seven-year Long-life warranty is the enthusiast's dream. A well-chosen older car may only need mechanical and cosmetic work to bring it back to its showroom glory. That is a lot easier than recovering the structure from a rusty hulk! On all post-1980 models the entire bodyshell was galvanised on both sides to a thickness that varies from 7.5 to 20 microns (millionths of a mm). On the 944, certain of the cavities are sprayed with wax preservative and all the models have pvc underbody coatings.

We will not spend any time on body panel recovery or replacement, you should read one of the more specialised texts for advice in this task. This is where I plug my own and Lindsay Porter's *Porsche 911–Guide to Purchase and DIY Restoration*, which, though about Porsche's rear-engined car will answer most questions on the techniques needed for a full restoration. Some general points will be made here on bodywork care and maintenance.

PAINTWORK CARE

There are two golden rules of paint-work care that every Porsche owner should pay attention to. The first is to wash the car regularly and often following certain rules and the second is to fix paintwork damage as soon as it is found. If you do this, the paintwork will stay in showroom condition for many years and that means a better resale value.

Firstly, let's consider new paint care. It's important to protect the paint layer from chemical and other attack. When the car is new, it should not be taken to an automatic car wash, as the paint may not have fully hardened and micro-scratches can be made on the surface. If the car is dusty, the brushes can also drag the dirt across the paintwork and scratch it further. The solution is to clean the car manually with lots of clean water and using a soft natural sponge. It may take longer but hand-washing is the only way to be sure that the paint stays in good condition. Micro-scratching can be particularly noticeable with black or the darker non-metallic colours.

The car should only be washed when the temperature is above freezing level. Use a high pressure hose to wash out the wheel wells and the underbody debris traps. The objective is to keep water away from the body in freezing conditions. If moisture freezes inside a stone-chip or paint crack, it will expand and flake the paint. Alternatively, it can cause micro-cracking over the whole surface, which leads to the 'dead' surface mentioned below. When the car is washed in cold weather, completely dry the paintwork with a clean chamois leather afterwards. At the end of the cold season, accept that the car must have a spring-clean and aim thoroughly to wash and inspect it.

Take a close look at the front section and underbody for flaking PVC sealer. When this is found, chip it back and use a phosphoric acid-based rust dissolver before priming and repainting. If a body sealer is used to repair chipped underbody protection, do not use the black tar-based underseal, it does not cure and looks very amateurish on a Porsche. Use an aerosol-applied pvc sealer for small areas and paint over the cured sealer with body colour later. Wurth are the recommended after-market supplier in Europe. Their aerosol body sealer is called Body Seal Spray, Part No.892 021 or (for larger areas) Wurth Stoneguard and Anti-Corrosion Compound, Part No.890 031 (grey) or 032 (ivory). Wurth can also supply a spray applicator for the latter items. Using these methods, the repair will be almost undetectable.

Another major factor in preserving the body colour pigment is the application of protective wax polish. This puts an oil base on the paint which not only helps to filter the sun's ultra-violet rays, but also protects the paint more in car washes. The car should not be washed using a detergent if this wax protection is to be maintained and only soap-based car shampoos should be used.

The orange-peel effect is not seen so much on later models as the quality of paint application has improved. The rippled effect was due to the paint mist partially drying before contact with the surface, so preventing satisfactory flow. The peel can be removed by cutting with rubbing compound but is probably best left, because this cutting will remove the hard outer skin of the paint.

If the paint has 'died' or turned to a flat finish, it should be cut back using a rubbing compound, being

careful not to rub down to the undercoats. The surface should then be waxed to preserve it and washed only with non-oil dissolving car shampoos. Don't try and respray small areas of the top coat with an aerosol, because it will be virtually impossible to match and later feather in the new paint with the old. Get the job done properly by a specialist, who will repaint the whole panel, after removing all the nearby trim, etc.

The stone-chip protection is where the zinc-coating comes into its own. Zinc corrodes in preference to steel in the presence of water. The zinc oxidises sacrificially and in the process forms a layer over the small area of a stone chip. The oxidation products of zinc have a smaller volume than those of steel and consequently the paintwork does not 'bubble' in the way it will when covering steel cor-

rosion. This does not mean to say that chips should not be retouched with a paint stick. For continued protection and appearance, this is essential.

PRESERVATION
Wax-oil preservatives certainly make a contribution to the increased corrosion protection. They should be applied evenly to all body cavities, including the doors, but with care. Ensure that drainage holes are not covered by the wax, especially behind the engine splash wall, the doors and in the rear luggage compartment wells. These particular areas should also be kept clear of leaves and other debris. Debris behind the splash wall can result in leakage into the car through cracked body sealer (caulking). When cleaning out this area, check the sealer carefully for signs of cracking or penetration and replace if necessary.

The advice is to clean up the cavities, wheel wells, etc, before application of a preservative, to get maximum protection. You should also know that though wax-oil may smell like it will make your car last a hundred years, it will not stop already established corrosion. The wax-oil preservatives are effective at repelling moisture, but can collect grime very quickly. If your car is a concours contender, a trade-off between shining good looks and moisture defence will be necessary.

WELDING ZINC-COATED STEEL
Welding is a specialist job and requires a lot of practice to do properly (the only way to do it on a Porsche). If you do it yourself do observe all the relevant safety precautions.

Those who are replacing metal should follow the factory advice and only use a spot welder or an inert gas

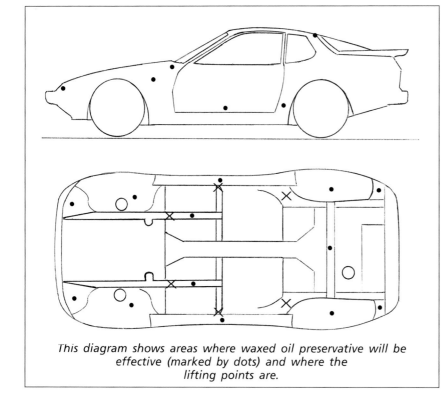

This diagram shows areas where waxed oil preservative will be effective (marked by dots) and where the lifting points are.

The foot of a lifting tower, placed on the front bodyshell rail. See how easy it is to catch the brake line, if the foot is placed carelessly.

arc welder (for instance, MIG) on clean, grease-free surfaces. In terms of preserving resale value, replace like with like, so if a steel wing comes off, replace it with another steel one.

The best approach when welding zinc-coated steel is to grind off the coating in the areas where the weld is to be made. Take care to remove the minimum amount of the zinc coating; the recommended spot weld size is 4–5mm. After welding, clean the seam with a wire brush and treat with a phosphoric acid-based rust dissolver, before spraying with an aerosol-applied pure zinc spray. The Wurth item is 'Zink-Spray', Part No.890111. The repaired area can then be painted with normal etch primer, etc.

BODY LIFTING POINTS
The lifting points are shown on the accompanying diagram. NEVER lift the car on a suspension member or an unsupported section of the bodyshell.

P A R T 2
DETAILS

There is not enough space to give an in-depth procedure for every item of bodywork trim removal, but I've chosen a number of items that are more commonly removed. Most things will be straightforward to dismantle, because the method of fixing will be clear. Look for the little caps which cover the mounting screws for interior trim and develop a feel for where items are clipped in place, rather than screwed. Most importantly with interior parts, make sure your hands are clean before touching them.

Above: *Door trim with manual window winder.*

Left: *The little plastic caps can be levered off to reveal a fitting screw. Lock pins simply unscrew.*

REMOVAL OF DOOR TRIM

If the car has wind-up windows, lift off the cover on the winding lever and remove the fitting screw, noting the original position of the winder. The door lever is backed by a plastic moulding and this must be prised out. Remove the screw that holds the surround plate around the lever and lift the surround away also. Remove the screws that hold the door pocket to the armrest and remove the pocket. Find the cap-headed bolts which hold the armrest to the door shell. Remove these and lift the armrest off. Remove the plastic caps that cover the fitting screws for the top ornamental strip next to the glass and unscrew the screws. Unscrew the door lock pin and remove this, followed by the strip. The lower section of the trim is fixed to the door shell by snap-fittings. Go around the edge of the trim, inserting a flat bladed screwdriver near the locations of the clips and prise them out of the shell. The trim can now be lifted upwards

Insert a screwdriver under the recess indicated and the inner cover will pop out. The outer moulding can then be removed.

and off the door shell. If electric windows are fitted and there is no need to disconnect the wiring (for instance if the door is being treated with preservative) simply hang the trim to one side of the door with the wiring still attached. Removal of the trim will reveal the plastic door sheet, which retains moisture within the door shell. If this is ripped or missing, it should be replaced using non-porous

The door pocket is retained at it's lower edge on three recessed screws.

plastic sheeting, cut to shape. It can be held in place using plastic adhesive tape.

REPLACING THE DOOR LOCKS

For one reason or another it may be necessary to replace the exterior door handles, including the locks. The accompanying photograph shows a door handle assembly. It is not necessary to remove the interior door trim to replace the exterior handles. Pull away the rubber door surround in the area close to the door handle, to reveal a small socket head bolt. Remove this and then slide the handle assembly forwards to free the rear part and then pull it back to disengage the front end from the door skin. With a screwdriver, carefully prise off the socket that operates the latching mechanism. The lock barrel may now be replaced. When taking out the barrel, leave the key in the lock to stop the assembly falling apart. If the barrels on the doors are changed, don't forget the rear opening tailgate lock, so that you keep one key for all the exterior locks.

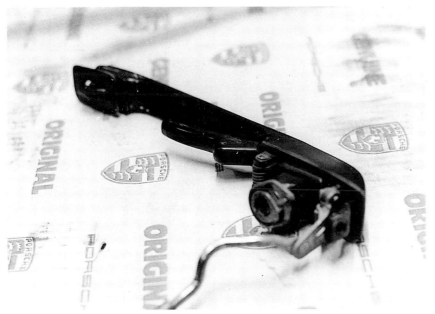

A door handle removed. The lock barrel is now easily changed.

63

To get access to the screw which holds the exterior door handle, peel back the seal a little.

FITTING A PASSENGER DOOR MIRROR

This description is suitable for both 924 and 944, assuming that both have an electric driver's door mirror fitted already. The circuitry and wire colours are identical. This is not a straightforward job and will take eight to ten hours to do properly. If you have any doubts, leave the work to a specialist. To fit the mirror, not only the passenger door trim has to be removed, but so will the driver's door trim, centre console and some of the carpeting. All the passenger door mirror parts can be bought as a kit, including the template and change-over switch and harness. The

mirror housing will need painting beforehand in the correct body colour.

Starting with the passenger door, stick strips of masking tape over the whole area where the mirror is to be mounted. This prevents accidental scratching and flaking of the painting during drilling and filing.

Top: *The passenger door mirror fitting on a RHD 924.*

Above: *The same mirror from the rear.*

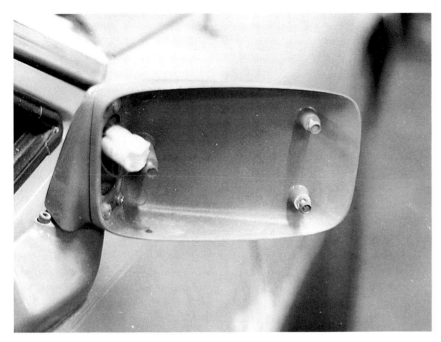

The reinforcement plate must be fitted inside the door skin, using pop rivets (which will be hidden later by the mirror body). Use this plate first as a template to drill the locating holes in the outer skin (see accompanying diagram). Always centre punch the hole positions, before drilling. File the holes out to the correct shape using a round metalwork file. At this stage position the reinforcing plate on the inside of the door skin and drill the holes for the pop rivets. Carefully remove the masking tape and fit the plate. Fit the mirror housing to the door and plug in its door harness.

Open the door as far as possible and pull back the flexible bellows that link the door to the pillar. This will reveal the other electrical leads to the door. At this stage, pull away

Top: *The painted mirror housing fitted, but with no internals in place.*

Above: *The mirror motor and flexible surround. Don't fit the mirror glass until everything else is finished, including testing. Note mirror heater wires.*

Right: *Hole positions in the passenger door for a RHD car (all dimensions in millimetres).*

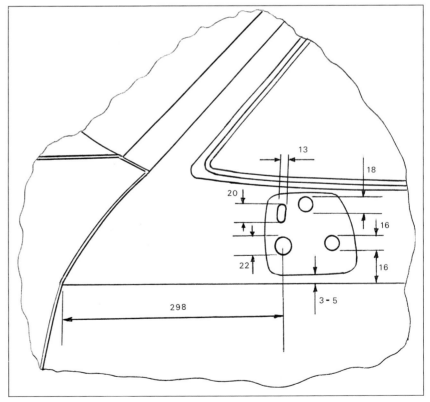

The front of the driver's door of a late model, showing flexible bellows and the rear glass release.

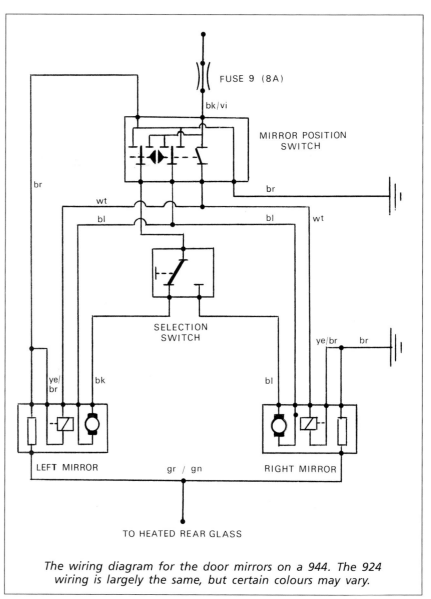

The wiring diagram for the door mirrors on a 944. The 924 wiring is largely the same, but certain colours may vary.

the sidewall carpet, just ahead of the door (if the car is RHD, then the bonnet release lever must be removed to do this). Run the new (mirror) harness down from the mirror and through the bellows into the area ahead of the door pillar.

Ensure that the new wiring in the door is well tucked out of the way and cannot foul the window mechanism. The second section of harness is shaped like a letter T. The arms of the T go across to each door, over the footwells, with the leg of the T coming forward to the location of the changeover switch in the centre console. In the area ahead of the passenger door pillar, plug the door harness and the T harness together. Tuck the harness over the footwells out of the way and use plastic cable clips to prevent it falling free. Bring the three wires that make up the leg of the

T back to the location of the changeover switch in the centre console (as shown in the wiring diagram). This switch is fitted just ahead of the ash tray and the trim will need lifting to hide the wiring. When this is completed, run the harness over the driver's footwell to the driver's door.

Pull back the driver's footwell

carpet (first removing the bonnet release, if necessary) and the door trim. Fit the new driver's door harness as shown and run the relevant leads down to the bellows and through into the area ahead of the pillar, ensuring it is well out of the way of the window mechanism. Complete the harness connections.

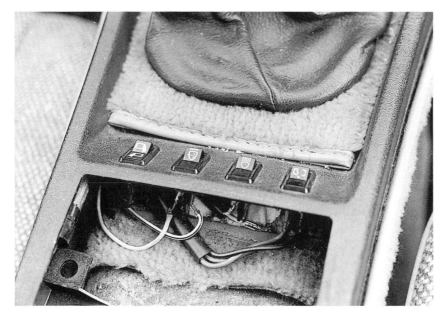

Above: *Cross-head screws attach the black plastic surrounds to the headlamp covers.*

Below: *The headlamp motor relay is located under a flexible boot next to the motor itself.*

With the ash tray removed, access to the central switches is straightforward. The mirror selector is on the left here.

Before refitting the trim and carpets, check the new mirror adjusts and warms up. The toggle switch should move each mirror in the same direction with similar movements.

REMOVING THE HEADLAMPS

Pop up the headlamps and turn the ignition off again. The black surrounds must first be removed by taking out the cross-head screws that attach them to the lid and the headlamp units. Sealed beam lamps are held by three cross-head screws to the pop-up frame and the electrical connection is made by a simple multipin plug. If the car has separate filaments, these must be unclipped from the rear of the headlamp assembly, once it is removed from the frame.

If replacing the headlamp, make sure it is the correct type for the model and that the beam dips the same way as the original.

Keep the mechanism that drives the headlamps up and down clean and well greased at its moving joints. The motor will last longer if its protective boot is pulled well down over the casing, so that moisture cannot get in. Where auxiliary headlamps are fitted into the bumper, these can be adjusted by turning the top or bottom mounting screws.

PART 3

CUSTOMISATION

Customisation can mean many things to many people. There are not that many Porsches on the roads, which makes the car fairly exclusive anyway. By customising, a totally individual statement can be made. There is no reason this cannot be done to a Porsche and the factory respond to the need for exclusivity that some customers have by offering a full bespoke service. At a (high) price the customer can specify one-off interiors, body styles or even full-race engines installed in outwardly standard bodies. The quality is better than factory production standards and some of the products have been breathtaking.

For most though, customisation is all about putting an individual identity on one's standard car within a set budget and enjoying the process of transformation. This could mean fitting spoilers and sill covers to a standard car or fitting a 944 Turbo engine and transmission to a 924 bodyshell (has anyone actually done this, I wonder?) Suffice it to say there is a great deal of opportunity for modification, especially with the 924, which can be taken out to full Carrera GTS specification or even (with a great deal of expense) very nearly go all the way to becoming a top specification 944.

Before we go further I must make a standard disclaimer. The modifications you do to your own car will be

at your own risk. You should always seek advice for any modification from a recognised specialist who, even then, may not accept responsibility for any parts or advice sold or given. It is very definitely a case of owner beware!

Most importantly, ensure that the basic structure of the car is sound before any modifications are made. Take advice on which areas should not be cut out or modified because they might affect the strength of the bodyshell. The fitting of fibreglass panels in place of steel ones cannot always be recommended for road use, because of the reduction in bodyshell stiffness. Modifying the car may make it more difficult to use and could compromise the car's safety. Note also that a modified car almost always does not realise the same resale value

as an original specification model. Any change that affects the bodyshell will nullify any outstanding manufacturer's anti-corrosion guarantee. Similarly, any mechanical changes will nullify any manufacturer's or subsequent guarantees.

Having said all that, customisation can be very satisfying, especially when the car is tastefully given a special identity and character that is unique. Think carefully about what you wish to do and plan the work out.

A 944 FROM A 924
Conversion of the 924 to the 944 shape is quite straightforward, but does require a fair degree of skill. If

A complete set of glass-fibre parts from Club Automobiles, to convert a 924 to a 944 lookalike. Buying them is the easy bit!

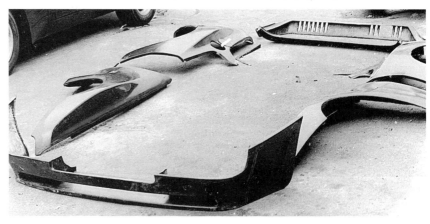

The front wings bolt on in place of the originals.

Above right: *The new rear wing perfectly blended into the old. After painting there are no signs of the join.*

Right: *The details around the rear threequarter window and fuel filler.*

no expense is spared all the 944 parts are available from Porsche. The cost of the conversion can be tailored to suit the pocket by the use of some or all glass-fibre items. Club Automobiles in Sparkbrook, Birmingham, England have been converting all types of Porsches for many years now. Indeed Richard Chilton, the proprietor, has successfully raced his idea of the 959, a heavily customised 911 that he developed during 1987/88.

His business offers a complete range of glass-fibre panels to convert the 924 into a 944 with relative ease. As the accompanying photographs show, the result is very impressive and will give a new lease of life to a hard-worked 924. The following will briefly discuss the steps of the conver-

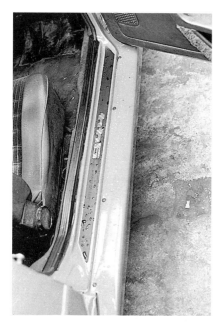

The body sill/rocker is fitted using self tapping screws.

wing panel is removed. The wing should now come off. Offer up the replacement panel to match the joining surfaces. Tidy up any rough joints or edges with a grinder and also grind off the zinc coating where welding is to be done (both on the new wing and the bodyshell). Use a spot welder. For the areas that are difficult to reach with the spot welder, use a MIG seam welder.

Left: *Black grommets cover the fitting screws and a factory decal finishes off the new look.*

Below: *The 924 bumpers are different to the 944's. Here Club Autos, snugly fit the smaller bumper inside the new 944 front air dam.*

sion, starting with notes on fitting rear steel panels. All the adjacent trim, including the rear three-quarter windows, rear lights and the front and rear bumpers will need to be removed before work can start on the full conversion.

The most difficult task is fitting the rear wings and this should be left to an experienced specialist. If steel is chosen, then the old ones must be carefully removed. This is done by first removing all the adjacent trim, the bumper and rear three-quarter glass and then drilling out the spot welds (using approx 6mm ($\frac{1}{4}$ inch) high speed steel drills). The cut line at the rear is the seam down from the rear opening window to the lights, where the seam will be visible. Look inside the rear compartment for the weld locations. Drill out the outer wing welds all around the wheel arch, door support and around the window. It may be necessary to cut

along the roof gutter line and then chisel off the remainder. Pull off the rear window rubber seal and drill out the spot welds along this section. It takes a lot of time but the wing should now come off. If the car is post 1980, disconnect the line to the integral fuel expansion tank as the

Use clamps to attach the new panel in place and be careful to get the correct position before welding. Once the welding is complete, tidy up the welds with a grinder and lead-fill the joints if necessary. Alternatively, use a good quality epoxy resin filler for this, but allow sufficient curing time before painting, to allow for filler shrinkage. Clean up the seams and exposed metal, using a phosphoric acid-based rust dissolver. Spray the exposed steel with a cold zinc spray, as mentioned earlier in this chapter. Take a lot of care to ensure good surface preparation. To ensure that there are no leaks from the wheel arches, seal the joints in this area with a curing sealing compound.

The front wings are much easier to attend to since they are bolted in place. Use a seam sealer between the wing and the mounting, to reduce moisture and vibration transfer (Wurth make 'Body Sealing Tape', part No. 890 100030 – it comes on

Expanded polyurethane foam is used by Club Autos to fill out the gap between the original steel rear wing and the new one. This helps cut down drumming also.

Right: *Note how the lower rear skirt has been blended to the 924 bumper.*

a roll and is grey-coloured). Spray the arches with the correct underseal as also discussed earlier. This will give a stippled finish that should then be primed again and painted as normal.

A factory polyurethane front spoiler can be fitted, but should only be painted with the recommended flexible paints or cracking will occur. Note that the bumpers on the 944 are different to those on the 924 and the front and rear will need modification if these are retained (see below). Alternatively, the front bumper can be forgotten if a 944 Turbo-style integrated front section is

The rear skirt from the back, showing the opening for the standard 924 exhaust tailpipe.

used. The factory method of attaching the sill extensions is to use self tapping screws and these are satisfactory for the rear skirt also. The rear window spoiler can be attached to the metal surround, using the same self tapping screws, but be careful during the drilling of the frame not to damage the glass.

Left: *The transformation is complete! Extra details include '944' rear logo and rear spoiler.*

Opposite bottom: *More details that improve the appearance include side repeaters (if not originally fitted) and the late style door rubbing strip. Only the four-stud wheels give it away that this is not a 'real' 944.*

GLASS-FIBRE BODY PARTS

Replacing the wings with glass-fibre items will probably take just as long, but be cheaper. It is definitely a specialist job, requiring a lot of skill to do well. Club Automobiles leave the standard 924 rear wings in place, so as not to reduce the bodyshell stiffness. The fibre-glass wing is fitted at its front edge by effectively creating a shallow step in the original steel wing that runs from the front lower edge of the three-quarter window down to the sill, following the line of the door shut and about 50 mm (2 in) back from it. This forms a recessed area into which the new wing can be fitted. Once the panels have achieved a satisfactory fit, they are fixed using either steel countersunk rivets or self-tapping screws. The

rivets should be used on all the seams that would be welded if a steel replacement panel were being fitted. The same attachment method is used for the rear section of the wing, either at the vertical seam with the rear panel, under the opening glass or alternatively, just ahead of the light cluster. If wider wheels are to be fitted, the original steel arches will need to be rolled back to give satisfactory clearance.

Once fitting is complete, the seams are all filled using a high-quality body filler. Allow a week for the filler to fully cure before flatting down.

Front view shows off how well the 924 bumper has been blended into the new air dam.

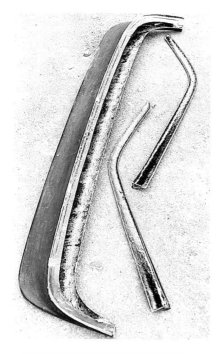

Top left: *Glass-fibre components of a 944-style rear spoiler.*

Top right: *The spoiler is fitted using self-tapping screws, through the window frame.*

Left: *Fitting screws at the side.*

Above: *This 924 has a German aftermarket flexible spoiler fitted.*

This time will allow any sinks to show up, due to shrinkage of the filler on hardening. Club Automobiles then fill the cavity between the glass-fibre and original steel rear wings with expanded polyurethane. This is injected into the cavity and conforms to the internal shape, it also seals the cavity from road spray and prevents panel resonance. Another method might be to fit a glass-fibre panel over the wheel arch aperture between the two wings.

Mick Phillips of Club Automobiles takes two working days to complete a full conversion, without painting. This includes front and rear wings, front and rear spoilers, sills and rear underbody spoiler, all in glass-fibre.

The standard 924 bumpers can be used with this conversion. The front wings are trimmed slightly so that the squarer 924 bumper clears the 944 wing shape. Similarly at the rear, the standard 924 bumper is retained with material being trimmed off the bumper's lower edge to enable the lower edge of the wing to be fitted. The accompanying photos show this best. For painting, they use a 2-pack self-etch primer and then either a 2-pack solid top coat or metallic base coat and lacquer. The enthusiast could consider using cellulose for a home respray, but this is only suggested if you have experience of this type of paint and understand its safe use. It is highly flammable. Club's package is completed by Compomotive 7 inch rims, side trim strips and '944' logos on the rear and on the door sills. The transformation from the mild-mannered 924 is complete!

CHAPTER 5

ENGINES

This chapter has been split into two parts covering the major engine types fitted to the 924 and 944. The aim in each section has been briefly to describe the general layout of the engines and their modified variants. This leads into a practical discussion about the good and bad points of the reliability, maintenance and problem identification.

924 ENGINE

The engine package selected by Porsche's engineers for the 924 owed everything to an original specification proposed by VW-Audi. The in-line four cylinder water-cooled engine delivered 125 bhp in standard 924 form. It was Porsche's racing engineers that showed that it could be significantly developed beyond the wildest dreams of the original Audi designers.

Left: *A general view of the 2-litre 924 engine.* 5p49

The engine block may have been used by VW in the LT van, but we should not forget that in heavily modified racing form the engine produced very respectable performances at Le Mans in 1980. The 'customer' Carrera GTR of the following year boasted no less than 375 bhp from the same parentage and still with a capacity of just 2-litres. This race-proven robustness goes a long way to explaining why the standard 924 has a very good reputation for reliability.

The configuration of the engine is conventional for a design originating in the late sixties/early seventies. The engine uses the well-proven crossflow cylinder head principle. The combustion chamber surface of the cylinder head is entirely flat, with the valves opening into a recess or bowl in the pistons. This 'Heron' head design allows the designer to stand the valves in a single line and operate them directly from the single overhead camshaft, without the need for any rocker linkage.

The crankshaft is supported in five bearings and a toothed belt drives the camshaft. The engine uses a wet sump lubrication system, with the oil pump driven directly off the front of the crankshaft. To fit it to the 924, the engine is canted over on its exhaust side which makes the Bosch K-Jetronic fuel injection system easily accessible on top of the block. Unfortunately the spark plugs are on the exhaust side of the cylinder head and are difficult to get at without the right tool. The oil filter, mounted below the exhaust manifold is only removable from under the car.

The relative simplicity of the engine is a bonus for the enthusiast, because the engine only has to be removed for the most major overhaul work on the block.

It is difficult to summarise what is meant by average usage for any engine, but assuming correct servicing and an absence of excessively hard driving, the 2-litre engine can be expected to give 80–100,000 miles of operation before a major overhaul will be necessary.

A top-end rebuild might be needed as early as 50,000 miles, to replace worn valve guides (see below), but this can be postponed by proper servicing. These figures can be shortened on the 924 Turbo, where the valves have a harder life, especially if the oil is not changed regularly.

VIBRATION AND CAMSHAFT WEAR

No balancing shafts are fitted to the 924 engine and consequently the unit can be described as harsh. The level of vibration has led to strengthening of several brackets and components during the 924's life (notably the air conditioning unit brackets). The most important vibration casualty in the engine is usually the camshaft oil feed tube. At each major service, when the valve clearances are checked, the condition of the tube (located above the camshaft) should be checked. At its rear end the bar is unsupported and can fracture due to the vibration. The result can go undetected (the broken piece usually falls to the side of the camshaft cavity), but the rear two cam lobes wear much faster due to poor lubrication. The wear can affect the camshaft and the valve tappets.

The camshaft itself should not reveal any cracks or excessive grooving (spalling) on the lobes. If there is a serious problem with the camshaft it should not repaired, but replaced. The noses of the camshaft lobes are

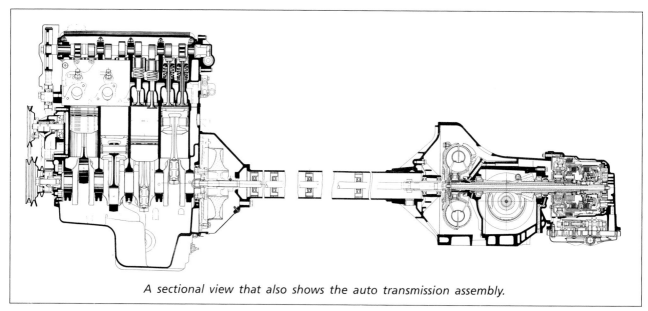

A sectional view that also shows the auto transmission assembly.

probably the most mechanically demanding places in the engine for the oil. For minimum wear, an oil film should be maintained at all times in this area of highest contact pressure between the components. If the oil is excessively contaminated or had not been changed for a long time, it will not be able to provide the support needed to keep the components from contacting each other. Heavy wear will quickly occur in this situation.

On US models, a compromise between performance and emissions was necessary with the camshaft design. The result was that on the pre-1977½ model, camshaft life was not as good as on the European model. The problem was that the valve opening angles, particularly on the inlet valve, were shortened but the lift stayed the same. This resulted in a sharper nose radius on the cam lobe, which led to heavy wear on the face of the lobe.

The post 1977½ US models were given the same opening angles (although different timing) as the European versions and these cams were expected to last to the first major overhaul, given correct oil changes. The other general factor to remember is to use good quality high performance oil, not a cheap supermarket brand.

VALVES AND VALVE GUIDES
Valve clearances are adjusted mechanically on the 924. A special tool should be used (Porsche tool W165) which is a socket key suitable for fitting to a 0.25 inch ratchet drive. This driver is available from Porsche as tool W166, but a normal ratchet drive will do, with a 3 mm socket driver to locate into the valve adjusting screw. If the ratchet handle can be bent through about 30 degrees, this will help access to the screw.

A sharp radius on the camshaft lobes demands regular oil changes, if problems are to be avoided.

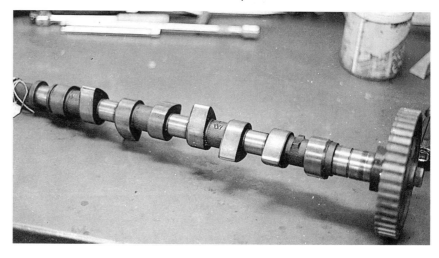

The socket key tool necessary to adjust the valve clearances.

When the clearances are checked on a cold engine, the inlet should be 0.10 mm (0.004 in) and the exhaust should be 0.40 mm (0.016 in). When the engine is warm the figures are 0.20 mm (0.008 in) and 0.45 mm (0.018 in) respectively. One complete turn of the adjusting key alters the valve clearance by 0.05 mm (0.002 in).

The symptoms of worn guides are an engine which is using more oil than usual and blowing blue smoke under hard acceleration. When the engine is idling and warm, the sound of the camshaft operating the valves will be easily apparent with the

A pair of 924 bucket tappets, showing the threaded part where the adjusting wedge screw fits.

bonnet open. Replacement of the guides is a specialist job. New guides make a remarkable difference to the noise level of the engine. Although the workshop manual tolerances are quite large, for quiet operation the guides should be replaced if a perceptible side-to-side movement can be detected when the valve is held by the stem just off the seat.

If the valves are removed from the head, number each one keeping it with its tappet. The exhaust valve seats are also prone to burning and if these are recut, then new tappet adjusters will also be needed.

GENERAL INFORMATION

If the head has been removed from the engine, check the bores for marking and evidence of blow-by past the piston rings. This latter could suggest the rings need replacing, especially if the engine is blowing oil yet the valve guides are in good condition.

The timing belt is not as critical on the 924 as the 944, but should be changed every 30,000 miles as preventive maintenance. Tensioning is a lot simpler than the 944 engine and can be done without special tools. The belt is at the right tension when it is just possible to twist it through 90 degrees at the mid-point between the cam and crankshaft pulleys.

The engine mountings of the 924 have none of the sophistication of the 944 items. The flexible mountings should be checked periodically for signs of splitting or perishing. They should not be covered in any oily deposits as this will shorten their life.

ENGINE SPECIFICATIONS

The engine specifications differed on the early model 924s from market to market and this information can be useful in identifying a car of unknown history. The factory engine

codes for these various model types were as follows:

924XH = USA and Canada models from launch.
924XG = USA, Canada and Japan, 1977½ models onwards.
924XF = California and Japan models from launch.
924XE = California and Japan, 1977½ models onwards.
924XK, XJ = Right-hand drive models.

924 TURBO ENGINE

There were major differences in the engine design of the 924 and 924 Turbo that have been briefly described in the introductory chapters. The turbo on the European models at launch was a KKK type K26-2470 R6. US models were fitted with type K26-2664 G 4.10. From 1981, the turbo was the same in all

The '931' part of the serial number on this casting shows it to be a Turbo head. Access to the plugs was much better than the original 924.

markets, being the type K26-2660 GA 4.10. The later Carrera GT used a different turbo again, type K26-2660 GA 6.10.

The common factor that all the turbocharged 924 models have is that they need a lot of care to extend the turbo life beyond about 40,000 miles. In some cases turbos have been known to need replacing as early as 25,000 miles. The main problem is that conventional mineral oils are not really suited to the very harsh temperature environment inside the casing of the turbo. The situation is satisfactory whilst the engine is running, but if shutdown occurs immediately after a hard run, the oil cooks in the turbo and on restart, the bearings wear badly. A worn-out turbo can be detected by smoke blowing from the exhaust, particularly as rpm increases. The only fix is to get the turbo reconditioned or replace it. From the 1981 models an improved crankcase breathing system promoted slightly better oil recirculation after shutdown.

The oil cooling problem was not effectively solved until the 944 Turbo arrived, with its water-cooled unit. The pre-1981 924 Turbo owner can retrofit the newer crankcase breather kit (although it is not an easy job) and all users should use a high performance oil (in the UK, try Shell Gemini) changing the lubricant at least every 6,000 miles. Another alternative is to use a fully synthetic oil (like Mobil 1), which has better temperature resistance to breakdown than a mineral-based oil and will not need to be changed so often. Engine oil should be changed regularly if only to prevent internal corrosion caused by the build-up of acidic by-products of combustion. This especially applies to engines that are not used very often.

Coming back to general handling

of a turbo, adopt the technique of letting the car warm up for a few minutes before pulling away from cold. This lets the oil warm and fully coat the unit's bearings, before it is asked to spin at its peak speed. After a hard run, let the engine idle for a few more minutes, to get the extreme heat out of the turbo and introduce a cooler, fresh oil supply.

Although not a very precise measurement of what is happening in the turbo, you can get an idea of the oil temperature in the sump by fitting a standard VDO oil temperature gauge. This fits in place of the clock in the centre console and the sender fits in place of the dipstick. The VDO part number for this is 323.801.014.001 and the kit comes with complete instructions for its easy fitting.

The cylinder head on the 924 Turbo is a wholly Porsche design, with no Audi ancestry. For improved combustion chamber efficiency, larger exhaust valve sizes were adopted and the spark plug relocated to the intake side of the chamber. The combustion chamber was

A cleaned-up Turbo head shows that these valve seats need some work.

The mechanical adjustment on the 924 and Turbo tappets is difficult to get at. It comes with practice!

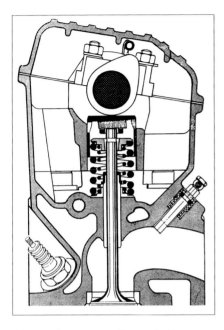

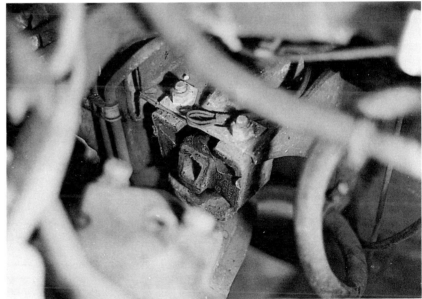

Above: *A cutaway through the cylinder head shows the wedge-shape valve tappet adjuster common to all 2-litre engines.*

Above Right: *Access to the turbo/manifold bolts is awful! It's easier to take the head off first, but don't cut too many of those braided lines. The ones with threaded ends are very expensive to replace.*

Right: *Simple, but reliable a 924 Turbo engine mounting.*

redesigned with a recess in the head as well as the pistons, to provide a lower compression ratio (7.5 : 1) than the unblown engine. If the head has been removed, check closely for signs of cracking, especially between the valve seats, as well as all the regular inspection points. Lubrication to the camshaft was improved although the manually adjusted tappets remained. The camshafts should be closely inspected for wear, especially near the nose of the cam. As with the standard 924, check also that the spray bar that runs across the top of the camshaft is not fractured (like the one in the accompanying photographs).

If the turbo is to be removed, it will be easier if the head is removed first, since access to the turbo/exhaust manifold nuts and bolts is virtually impossible otherwise.

PART 2

944 ENGINE

ENGINE LAYOUT

The 944 engine is much more complex in design than its 2-litre 924 counterpart. The 944 engine should not be taken apart unless the right tools are available and you have an understanding of the design. The following discussion will concentrate on the single-camshaft 2.5-litre engine.

The 2.5-litre four cylinder engine, fitted with all its ancillaries.

The crankcase is a complex two-part aluminium alloy design with no separate liners (the pistons are iron-sprayed). The main upper section is heavily ribbed to improve stiffness and reduce the chance of resonant vibration, excited by the moving parts. The lower section, or 'ladder', is another casting, which supports the main bearing caps and gives additional stiffness to the crankcase. The sump casting also contributes to the overall rigidity of the engine, again being heavily ribbed and attached to the upper block casting by a remarkable 22 bolts.

As described in Chapter 2, engine vibration is significantly reduced by the two balance shafts, one either side of the block, running at twice engine speed.

The cylinder head is attached to the block by ten studs that are fitted to the top of the machined block

casting. The camshaft cover does not merely act as a cover over the valves, but retains the camshaft itself and contributes to the stiffness of the upper section of the engine. The camshaft runs in its housing without bearings. The hydraulic tappets do not require adjustment as part of normal servicing.

There are three rows of drive belts driven from the front of the crankshaft. The toothed belt closest to the block runs at half engine speed and is the drive to the camshaft and the water pump. The next one out is the double-toothed belt which drives the balance shafts, mentioned earlier. The third pulley drives the alternator using

82

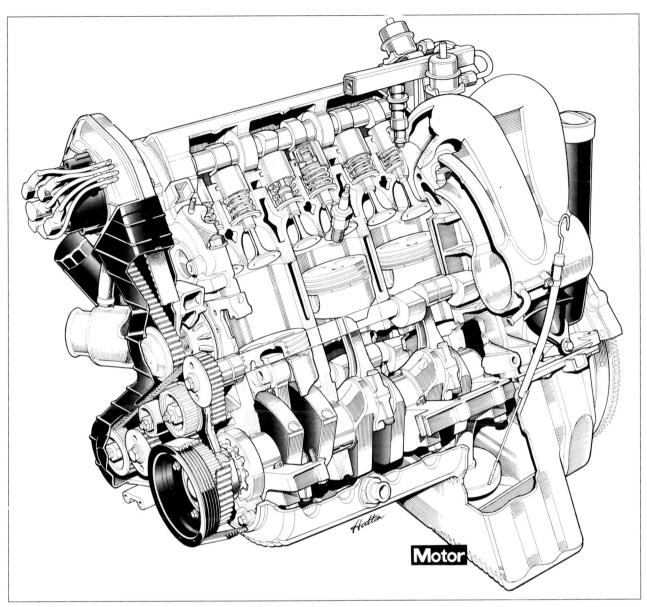

Motor

a 'poly-rib' belt. If power steering is fitted then a drive for the pump is taken off another pulley, fitted in front of the alternator pulley.

A feature of the 944's oil system is the oil/water intercooler. This speeds up the warming of the oil when the engine is cold and takes heat out of the oil when the engine is hot. The design eliminates the need for a separate oil cooler. The crankcase also contains a complex oil separator and ventilation system. The oil consumption is given as acceptable up to 1.5 litres per 1000 km (234 miles/Imp pt or 388 miles/US qt), but a good engine should do much better than this.

A cutaway view of the 2.5-litre engine. Note the oil pump located on the front of the crankshaft, behind the drive pulleys. (Courtesy Motor)

PORSCHE 924

The crankshaft and its supporting
'ladder' casting.

One of the two balance shafts.

Left: *The complex sump casting.
Note the ribbing to reduce oil
surging.*

Above: *The pistons are iron-
sprayed and have one oil scraper
and two compression rings.*

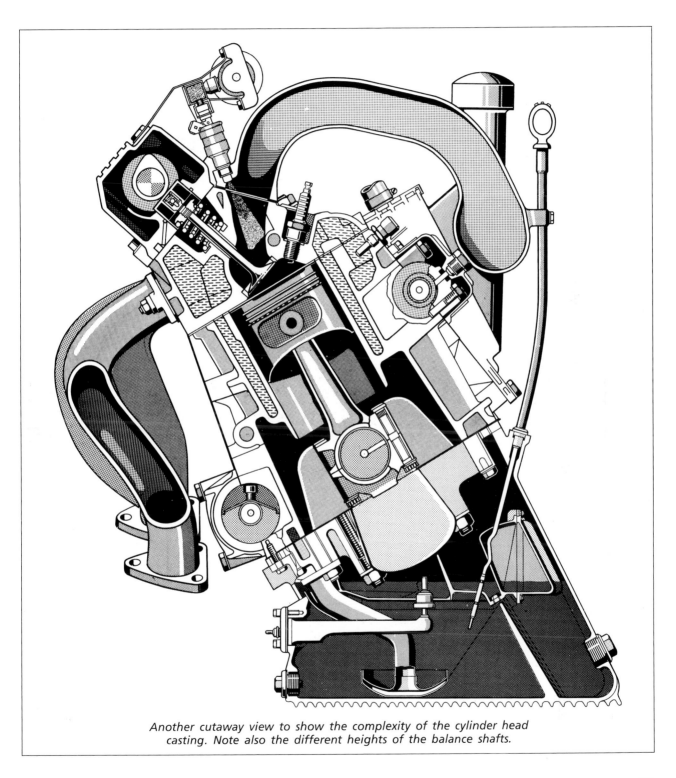

Another cutaway view to show the complexity of the cylinder head casting. Note also the different heights of the balance shafts.

A new cylinder head with the valves installed.

Above right: A busy place! This view of the front of the sixteen-valve engine shows the four separate drive belts driven from the crankshaft. Note also the automatic tensioner for the timing belt.

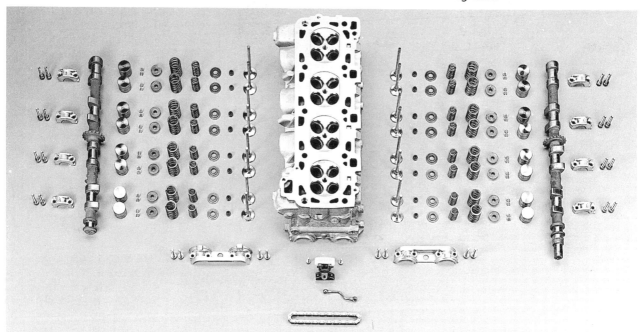

A sixteen-valve head stripped down to its lowest level. The inlet camshaft is driven from the exhaust camshaft by the small simplex chain.

The oil/water intercooler and its housing, showing the filter.

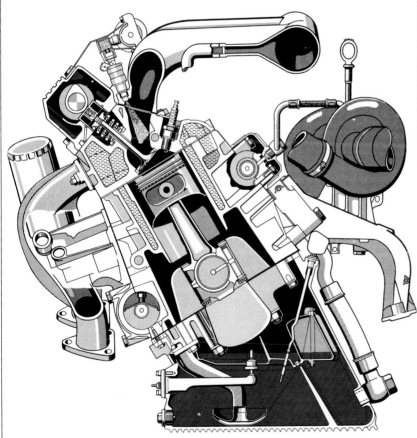

The 944 turbocharger is located on the left side of the engine, the same position as previously seen on the 924 Carrera GTR.

TURBOCHARGING

The turbocharger installation of the 944 Turbo is a significant technical advance on the 924 Turbo. The key mechanical feature is the inclusion of water cooling in the turbocharger body, to prevent the lubricating oil from overheating after shutdown.

The second coolant circuit is controlled by an additional thermostat, which opens at the same temperature as the main engine thermostat (about 82°C). An additional water pump in the turbocharger coolant circuit draws coolant from the main expansion tank, which then flows through the turbocharger circuit. An additional temperature switch is also positioned in the coolant return line from the turbo and, after engine shutdown, if the coolant temperature rises to approximately 115°C, the electric pump will switch on in the turbo circuit. Note that after shutdown this secondary coolant circuit is a closed loop between the turbo and the expansion tank. The expansion tank has a check valve to prevent the coolant from flowing back to the turbo.

The electric pump is always switched on for 25 seconds every time the engine is stopped, regardless of how high the coolant return flow temperature is.

GENERAL INFORMATION

Because the engine uses aluminium castings extensively, which are easily damaged or scratched, good working practice is essential when handling the parts.

Most important is cleanliness: with aluminium bores and many direct mating faces, allowing debris to get on the parts during assembly must be carefully avoided. The result of trapped debris could be excessive oil leaks, or even worse, marked bores. Before removing any part of the

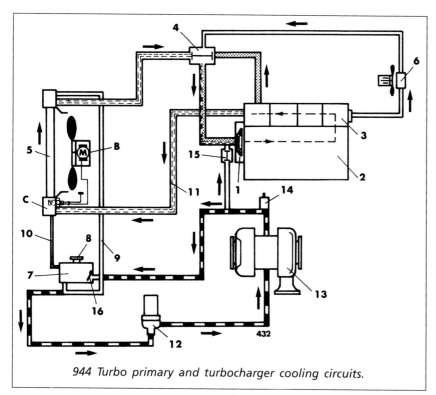

Legend 1 Water pump
2 Crankcase
3 Cylinder head
4 Thermostat
5 Radiator
6 Heat exchanger
7 Expansion tank
8 Filler neck
9 Filling line
10 Vent line
11 Return line
12 Electric pump
13 Turbocharger
14 Temperature switch
15 Additional thermostat
16 Check valve
B Electric fan
C Temperature switch

944 Turbo primary and turbocharger cooling circuits.

Cleanliness is absolutely vital. The aluminium bores are very easily damaged.

A virtually stripped engine casting. The water pump is closest to the camera.

engine, the whole unit should be washed down with a grease-dissolving cleaner. Note how clean the parts of the engine are in the accompanying photographs.

The major castings of the engine are all matched and numbered. Because the seating of each casting on its neighbour is critical, each casting is identically numbered to prevent the parts getting mixed up in a busy engine shop. The main castings (except, of course, the cylinder head to the block) are assembled without gaskets and only the recommended sealer should be used, which allows the component faces to actually contact each other and so be positioned exactly, yet form an oil seal. The sealant is not like a conventional liquid or instant gasket, being thinner in consistency. In Europe the recommended sealer between the crankcase and the ladder is Loctite 574 and between the crankcase and the balance shaft housings is Loctite 638. The correct surface cleaning and application of both of these sealers is critical for a good engine rebuild. Outside Europe, consult your Official

It is important not to mix up the castings. Note the number stamped on this balance shaft housing, which will match that stamped on the other major casting.

Good practice seen here by marking the piston number and its orientation on the crankshaft.

The consequences of a poor engine rebuild can be dramatic, as this con rod shows.

Porsche Centre for the right sealer, if Loctite is unavailable.

The need to provide exact positioning means engine oil should not be used for this sealing function as this will hold the castings apart, even when tightened down. The importance of this gasketless assembly can be demonstrated on the assembly of a balance shaft to the main block. Overtightening can cause the shaft to bind in its bearings and too thick a sealant layer, using for instance new engine oil, will result in a loose shaft fit. This would mean a noisy engine, rapid bearing wear and a leaky engine. This is a good way of establishing how proficient a garage is. Just ask them how they assemble their engines.

New engine oil should be used for coating the bearing faces, rings and bores, cam faces and other points of contact where protection is needed to prevent instantaneous damage on first start-up. A smear on the cylinder head studs will help prevent corrosion there.

Only new gaskets, oil seals and load bearing bolts (like those for the con rods and big ends) should be used on reassembly of a dismantled engine and note that certain nuts/bolts require a staged tightening sequence to seat the parts correctly.

ENGINE SPECIFICATIONS

The factory designations for the 2.5-litre 944 engine are as follows:

Europe, Rest of World	(manual)	to Feb 1985:	M44/01
Europe, Rest of World	(auto)	to Feb 1985:	M44/02
USA	(manual)	to Feb 1985:	M44/03
USA	(auto)	to Feb 1985:	M44/04
All markets	(manual)	from Feb 1985:	M44/05
All markets	(auto)	from Feb 1985:	M44/06

CYLINDER HEAD

Head gasket failure on a 944 can occur as a result of failure of the oil/water intercooler (difficult to detect by exterior visual inspection). The early intercoolers were thought to be critical on their alignment in the housing, so correct fitting was important. Latterly, the red oil seal rings have been considered to be at fault (maybe due to hardening) and these have been replaced by green seals. The green seals are the current best fit for the intercooler.

Another very expensive consequence of the oil and water mixing can be the destruction of the engine block. Unfortunately, this is the principal disadvantage of the linerless aluminium cylinders. If the oil/water mixing goes undetected, the oil cannot support the pistons in the bores correctly and heavy marking of the cylinders can occur. The only remedy, usually, is to scrap the block.

The oil/water intercooler showing its oil seal ring. There is another on the opposite side of the matrix.

Regular checking of the water temperature in normal driving will prevent serious damage, and if the temperature rises abnormally, check the exhaust for steam or water droplets and look for water on the dip-stick. If in doubt, get specialist advice.

Head removal should not be

The NTC2 (engine temperature) sensor for the L-Jetronic system is forward of the coolant temperature sensor. They are both mounted at the top-front of the engine block.

Above right: *Hydraulic tappets installed in the camshaft housing.*

Right: *A cylinder head ready for valve strip down. Note the clean work surface.*

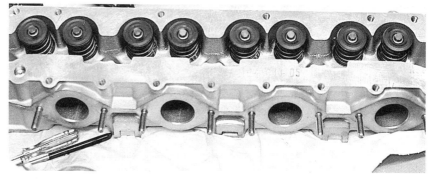

attempted unless you have a workshop manual and, most importantly, Porsche tool P9201 to set the belt tensions on reassembly.

When removing the camshaft housing, make a point of counting out the recessed bolts that fit the casting to the cylinder head, as they are taken out. These bolts are the ones under the aluminium plugs in the top of the casting. It is very easy to drop a bolt into the camshaft housing as it is loosened and forget it. You may only realise one bolt is missing when everything is reassembled again and complete disassembly will be necessary to retrieve the lost bolt. This can be a bit hard on the nerves. Take care also that the hydraulic tappets do not slip out of the camshaft housing as it is removed. With the camshaft housing

off, the ten nuts that retain the cylinder head can be removed. Refer to the 924 section of this chapter for a discussion of camshaft condition.

The combustion chambers and ports should only be cleaned chemically or with a tool that does not damage the aluminium (or ceramic in some cases). Be very careful not to scratch the valves as this can set up stress points later, which can lead to total valve failure. There should be no perceptible side play of each valve in its guide.

Inspect the combustion chamber, valve seats and guides very carefully, looking for cracks and pitting.

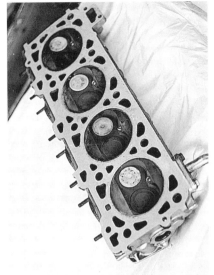

years some minor changes were introduced that improved cooling air supply to the right-hand mounting (a small heat shield between the exhaust manifold and the mounting and splash guard louvres). Improved mountings have been available from 1985, which are more robust items. These later mountings can be recognised by their painted bases (the latest is orange). The mountings are date stamped, but the easiest way to check if your car has them is to take it to an Official Porsche Centre for inspection.

The hydraulic engine mountings are filled with anti-freeze fluid and act like shock absorbers. They control low frequency vibrations by forcing

It's quite normal for a combustion chamber to be coated in black deposits and the exhaust valve to be a lighter colour. Pitting of the aluminium around the exhaust valve could suggest use of low grade fuel.

Above right: The combustion chambers and ports should be cleaned with a gentle abrasive or a chemical cleaner.

The tightening sequence for the cylinder head nuts. The front is to the left.

On reassembly, the head gasket should be tightened down in a set sequence. Note the tightening sequence shown on the accompanying photograph. Each nut should first be tightened to a torque of 20 Nm (15 lb ft) then increase the torque to 50 Nm (68 lb ft) and finally torque each nut to 85 Nm (115 lb ft). Leave the assembly for 30 minutes and loosen all the nuts one quarter turn and then retighten to 85 Nm. New timing and balance shaft belts should be used if the engine is being reassembled.

HYDRAULIC ENGINE MOUNTS

The technical details of these have been explained in Chapter 2. In practice their performance has been good, but there are certain points to be aware of.

Early models suffered failures of the right-hand engine mount due to overheating. During the 1983 model

the fluid repeatedly through a small opening between two chambers inside the mounting.

A failed mounting might be signalled by a heavy vibration at starting, shutdown or idle. The vibration tends to go away as the engine speed increases above about 1500 rpm. Before concluding that an

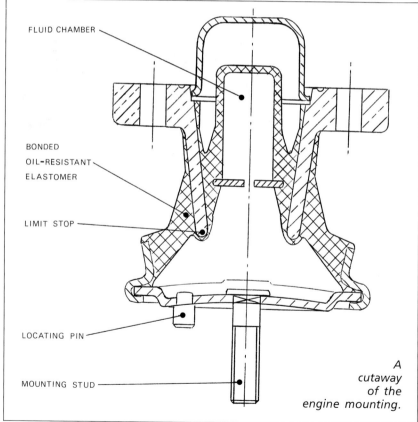

FLUID CHAMBER

BONDED
OIL-RESISTANT
ELASTOMER

LIMIT STOP

LOCATING PIN

MOUNTING STUD

*A
cutaway
of the
engine mounting.*

Above left: *The working environment for the right-hand mounting
is far harsher and has been the
side on which most failures have
occurred.*

Above: *The engine mounting on
the bench. Look for signs of fluid
leakage.*

Below: *The grey paint on the
lower part of this mounting shows
it to be the later improved type.
The very latest type – retrofittable
to all models – has an orange
identification stripe.*

This is what is should look like, when fully filled with fluid.

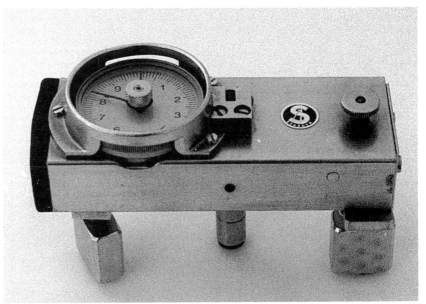

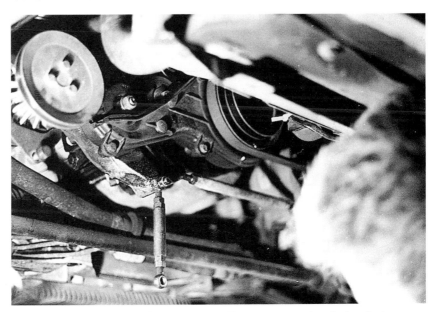

engine mounting is faulty, you should be sure that the fuel system is set up correctly. Running lean at low rpm when the engine is cold could give a lumpy idle which can feel like a vibration, but in this case it smooths out when the engine is warm. Another possible cause of such a vibration might be the balance shafts being wrongly adjusted, but the vibration caused in this way would not go away with increasing rpm. The mountings fail when the fluid leaks out and this can clearly be seen. The engine also sits lower on the failed side, which can cause gear selection problems. When the mounting is removed its height between the bearing faces should be no less than 65 mm (2.56 in) and when they are new they are 70+/-1 mm (2.76+/-0.04 in). The mounting has a metal cap on its top which can be (carefully) prised off to see whether the chamber is filled. The flexible bellows will be collapsed if the chamber has leaked.

DRIVE BELTS

The power steering and alternator belt tensions can be adjusted rela-tively simply by altering the length of two tie-rods, located near the bottom-front end of the block. These belts should be able to be deflected by about 5 mm (0.25 in) with a finger. To adjust the tension, loosen the lock nuts at each end of the tie-rod and turn the rod itself. Retighten

Top: *944 Porsche timing belt tension gauge. The scale is dimension-less.*

Above: *The power steering pump adjustment tie-rod hanging off to ease access to the balance shaft belt.*

93

To set number one piston at Top Dead Centre, line up the rib on the distributor housing with the groove in the camshaft pulley.

This view shows how the tension is measured, using here a balance shaft belt off the engine as an example.

Checking the balance shaft and timing belt tensions is a mechanic's nightmare. It must be done at every service!

the lock nuts when satisfied with the tension.

To check the condition of the balancing shaft drive belt, take the alternator tie-rod off at one end to remove the multi-vee belt completely. This gives access to the plastic cover over the double-sided belt. Remove the bolts that hold the cover all around its edge. Check the belt for fraying or other damage. If you don't have Porsche tool P9201 for checking the tension, do not remove or adjust the belt, leave it to a specialist.

To check the position of the balance shafts is correct, turn the crankshaft clockwise until the Top Dead Centre (TDC) mark on the cam-

If the belt is removed, check it closely for damage and signs of splitting at the base of each tooth form.

The measuring gauge on the timing belt. Reading it is also difficult!

shaft drive pulley aligns with the cast mark inside the small opening in the camshaft housing, next to the distributor cap. The TDC mark, 'OT' on the flywheel seen against the bellhousing reference mark must also be aligned. The marks on the balance shaft pulleys should be aligned with the reference marks on the rear of the toothed belt cover. If they are not consult a specialist.

TIMING BELTS

There has been some concern since the launch of the 944 about the reliability of the camshaft timing belt. With correct servicing the timing belt should give no problems.

The failure, when it has happened, has usually been tooth breakage as a result of insufficient tension, leading in the worst cases to slippage of

the camshaft pulley and contact of the valves with the pistons – a very expensive failure.

Pre-1984 models also suffered from timing belt teeth breakage due to contact (again from reduced tension) with a V-shaped strengthening web in the rearmost plastic moulding, behind the belt. The web was located between the water pump and camshaft pulleys. The web has been omitted from cars made after April 1984.

For a new belt the factory workshop manual originally gave a setting of 2.7 +/- 0.3, using tool P9201 with the engine cold (the scale used on the gauge is dimensionless). From 1985, the specification was changed to an initial setting of 4.0 and a new stronger belt was offered. The 1985 recommendation was that the tension must be adjusted again after

750-1500 miles (at the initial service), once the belt has completed its initial stretching. This has now been relaxed to 2000 miles. The 'post run-in' setting is the old figure of 2.7. After this, routine checking of the tension is advised every 12,000 miles. The belt is claimed to last the life of the engine. When resetting the belt tension, using the eccentric clamp and the measuring gauge, turn the engine over (by hand) several times after clamping and recheck the gauge reading, so that the belt tension is distributed equally. Your knuckles will take a beating whilst fiddling with the tensioner bolt!

If you still think you have the older, pre-1985, belt fitted and you know the service history, its condition and tension should be checked every 10–12,000 miles and it should be replaced around 30–35,000 miles by a new belt of the new type. If you don't know the history, change it now to the new type. With correct preventive maintenance, the timing belt will be trouble-free.

From the 1987 model year, the tensioning has been automatic, eliminating the need for the fiddly gauge on the timing belt. The ten- sioner clamping bolt is simply loo- sened, the engine manually turned over once or twice to balance the tension and then retightened.

A fine portrait of the standard 924 and 944

This colour cutaway of the 1983
924 shows well the general
configuration of the engine,
rear-postioned gearbox and suspension systems. Also to be
seen is the Berber interior trim.

The Porsche 924.

The Porsche 924 Turbo Carrera

The 2.5-litre turbocharged
Porsche 944 engine

The Porsche 944S. (Andrew Morland)

The latest, and perhaps, prettiest of the 924/944 range, the 944 cabriolet.

CHAPTER 6
FUEL SYSTEM

OUTLINE OF THE 924 SYSTEM

The fuel system components' complexities make for a heavy read, but I've tried to keep the description as short as possible. The easiest way to follow the description is to refer to the illustration. The Bosch K-Jetronic Continuous Injection System (CIS) is used on all models of the 924. A fault finding guide is given at the end of this section, but for detailed strip-down information use the Haynes Owners Workshop Manual on the 924 (Book No. 397).

The Bosch K-Jetronic fuel injection and ignition system as fitted to the 2-litre 924.

The system is entirely mechanical in operation, principally depending on the flow of air through a venturi and the position of a lifting (sensor) plate in that airstream to gauge the ratio of the fuel/air mixture. The accompanying figure shows the major components of the system. Air passes through the air filter, and past the air-flow sensor and on to the two throttle butterflies. From there, the air is distributed to each of the four inlet ports in the cylinder head. Directly above each inlet valve is located a fuel injector, which continuously sprays a mist of fuel, whilst the engine is running.

As the air passes through the air-flow meter, the sensor plate is lifted

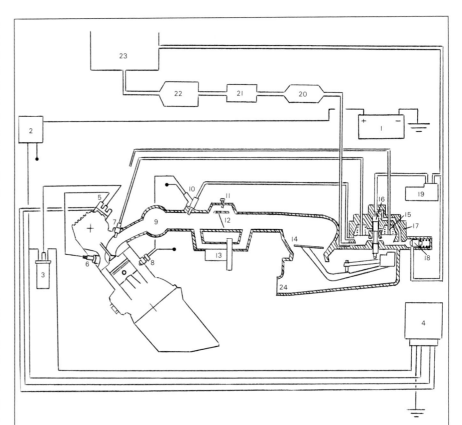

1 Battery	11 Bypass screw	19 Control pressure regu-
2 Ignition lock	12 Throttles (2)	lator
3 Ignition coil	13 Auxiliary air regulator	20 Fuel filter
4 Ignition control unit	14 Air sensor plate	21 Fuel accumulator
5 Distributor	15 Pressure regulating	22 Fuel pump
6 Spark plug (4)	valve	23 Fuel tank
7 Fuel injector (4)	16 Control piston	24 Air intake
8 Thermo-time switch	17 Fuel distributor body	
9 Air intake distributor	18 System pressure	
10 Cold start valve	regulating valve	

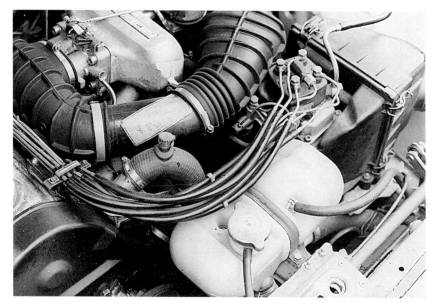

Important components of the K-Jetronic system are the metering unit (on the right with the pipe fittings) and the air distributor (with Porsche logo on top).

Right: *Close-up of the fuel metering unit on a 924 Turbo. Main fuel delivery pipe comes in from the side and indicated is the control pressure line, surrounded by the four injector feed pipes.*

to an angle dependent on the airflow (and therefore engine) speed. This movement is used to determine the amount of fuel required by the engine, assuming a fixed fuel/air ratio of 1:14.

As the diagram shows, the sensor plate is connected through a lever arm to a piston. This piston, located in the fuel distributor next to the sensor plate venturi, has a single, large piston ring-like groove machined into it, which controls the opening and closing of the ports in the wall of the bore. The ports connect the fuel delivery from the fuel tank to each injector. As the sensor

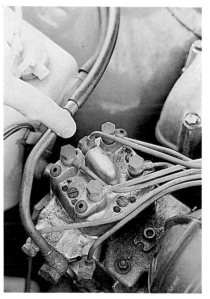

plate lifts in the inlet airstream, the piston lifts and more fuel is supplied to each injector. Fuel enters the lower section of the distributor body, and it then enters the piston bore to be distributed via four pressure regulating diaphragm valves to the ports leading to the injectors.

The ratio of fuel/air supplied by this

device would be an unsatisfactory straight line relationship dependent on engine speed. In real operating conditions the mixture needs to be slightly rich at idle, lean for constant speed and rich for hard acceleration. The straight line relationship is modified to the required shape, by altering the profile of the venturi. The changing load conditions are therefore accommodated by what appears as a slight wine glass profile. The shape of the venturi should not be modified by the enthusiast.

When the ignition is turned on, the pump supplies fuel via an accumulator and fuel filter, to the inlet side of the fuel distributor. The accumulator damps down fuel surge and helps maintain fuel system pressure after

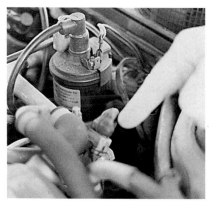

Cold-start valve in a 924 Turbo.

shutdown helping to prevent vapour locks. The amount of fuel needed is dependent on the position of the metering piston and excess is returned to the tank by the system pressure regulating valve. The fuel system pressure is approximately 3.45 bar (50 psi) and the regulating valve opens at 4.83 bar (70 psi). This valve, a simple spring-behind-a-piston device like an oil pressure relief valve, is located on the side of the fuel distributor. As the engine is turned by the starter, the airflow lifts the sensor plate to open the ports to the injector lines. The injectors open at a fuel pressure from 2.4 - 3.45 bar (35 - 50 psi).

Pressure is maintained on the top of the fuel metering piston by a secondary fuel circuit. The pressure of this secondary circuit is controlled by the control pressure regulator (or warm-up valve). It is fitted to the rear of the intake housing. Fuel enters the regulator from the area above the metering piston and there is a return line from it back to the tank. The regulator contains a valve, which is held open against a spring by a bi-metallic strip. When the engine is started current flows to the heater element and it bends with the spring force, closing the valve, until no more fuel flows. A cold engine and cold valve lets most of the fuel return to the tank. This results in a lower pressure on top of the metering piston, which moves higher in its bore. This gives more fuel to the injectors and a richer mixture. As the regulator (and engine) warms, its valve closes and the pressure on the top of the piston increases, reducing the fuel volume and giving a leaner mixture.

When the engine is started from cold, a fifth injector (or cold start valve) squirts neat fuel into the intake manifold for between 3 and 10 seconds. The injector is operated by a solenoid in the valve body, but the timing is controlled by the thermo-time switch, its bi-metallic strip operated contacts heated by the coolant system. It is located on the engine block.

The amount of air for slow idling with a warm engine is not enough for a cold start. The auxiliary air valve is connected with hoses to the air intake by the air cleaner and air distributor. It is a gate valve operated by (another!) bi-metallic strip.

The 924 Turbo throttle by-pass valve is behind the air distributor.

The pressure duct and throttle housing on the 924 Turbo. At the left is the charge pressure safety sensor, in the middle is the outlet from the throttle by-pass valve and the connector to the throttle housing on the right is the inlet air temperature sensor.

Hot starting is the weak area for early 924 models. The fuel accumulator should maintain system pressure for a short period after shutdown, to avoid vapour locks. A one-way valve was fitted after the fuel pump to post-1981 models and many owners have fitted these to earlier models. The slightest leak from the main fuel circuit will cause hot starting problems, because vapour locks will form.

924 FUEL SYSTEM

Firstly, consider a safety note. Remember that fuel vapour and sparks do not mix – the result could be lethal. The K- Jetronic system is not complex, but aside from the checks mentioned below, the advice is to leave problems to a specialist. Its efficient function depends on a fine balance of adjustments that should only be done with the correct equipment. I will not discuss here the mixture adjustment as this should be performed accurately with a CO meter. In the USA the mixture is the key adjustment for controlling emissions and should only be performed by a specialist. The required values for CO percentage volume are given at the end of the next section.

FUEL SYSTEM DIAGNOSIS

These tests check the fuel system pressures and fuel delivery rates. The easiest item to replace is often the last to get looked at, namely the fuel filter. Check this first, it can save a lot of time! It should be replaced every 30,000 miles.

To check the fuel control and system pressures you will need a pressure gauge that reads 0-7 bar (0-100 psi). The factory item is tool number P378. The gauge is used to search for fuel system leaks and pressure fluctuations and can be made up quite easily in the home workshop. The best improvisation I have seen uses a Schrader compression gauge (part number 8888RG). There are two pipes going into the gauge 'T' piece and each of these is trimmed to within about 225 mm (9 in) of the 'T'. Into one pipe-end the smaller thread of a brass union (Porsche part number 063133541) is screwed. Into the other pipe end push a short piece of fuel injection line (the section that joins the distributor to the control pressure regulator is ideal, either new or used) complete with the attachment point to the metering unit. The pipe junctions will need binding with small metal pipe-clips (Jubilee) or larger diameter rubber tubing. The connections need to be tight enough to prevent leakage when the finished piece of equipment is used, namely a simple clamp to compress the rubber pipe. The gauge must be fitted

between the fuel distributor and the control pressure regulator, replacing the control line.

If the car is having starting problems from cold, then the control pressure should be checked when the engine is cold. The gauge should be connected as described above and the clamp fitted to the regulator side of the gauge. With the warm-up regulator and the airflow sensor plugs disconnected, turn on the ignition and read the gauge. It should show 1.5 bar (22 psi) at 20°C. Note that this pressure is affected by ambient temperature. If the engine is warm the control pressure range should be from 3.4 to 3.8 bar (50 to 55 psi).

If the readings are outside the ranges, check the system for leaks and loose fittings, but otherwise the warm-up regulator should be replaced. If the pressure is well below this, the fault may lie in the pump or filter.

To check the system pressure, remove the clamp. Assuming the

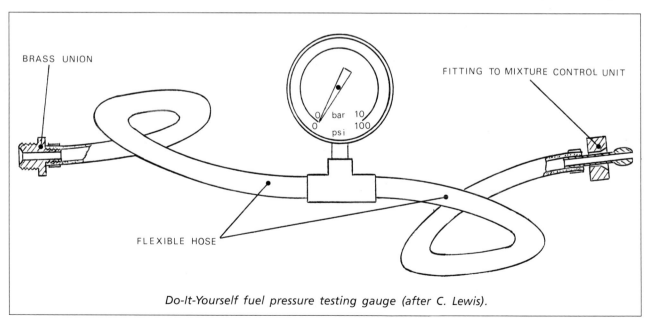

Do-It-Yourself fuel pressure testing gauge (after C. Lewis).

PORSCHE 924

Mixture adjustment screw.

pump and filter are in good condition, the gauge should read between 4.5 and 5.2 bar (66 to 76 psi). If the reading is outside this then the piston pressure regulator in the fuel distributor should be reshimmed.

From 1979 a safety circuit operated by the fuel pump relay was fitted (replacing the earlier safety contact on the airflow sensor). The circuit across the relay must be bridged to

Idle adjustment screw on the throttle housing (924 Turbo).

SUMMARY OF 924 FUEL SYSTEM DATA

Test	Specification
Fuel pump delivery rate	at least 750 cc in 30 seconds
Control pressure 'cold'	1.5 bar (22 psi) at 20 °C
Control pressure 'warm'	3.4 to 3.8 bar (50 to 55 psi)
System pressure	4.5 to 5.2 bar (66 to 76 psi)
Idle speed (rpm)	950 +/- 50
USA manual to 1977½ model	925 +/- 75
USA from 1981 model	750 - 800
Autos from 1981 model	1000 +/- 50
CO level (%):	
Europe	1.0 to 2.0
USA (1977½ - 78 excl Calif)	0.5 to 1.0*
USA (1979 excl Calif)	0.7 to 1.1*
USA (1980 incl Calif)	0.6 to 1.0
USA (from 1981 incl Calif)	0.5 to 1.0+
USA (1976-78 Calif)	max. 0.7
USA (1979 Calif)	0.8 to 1.2

All measured in front of catalytic converter.
  * measured with air pump and/or active carbon tank disconnected.
  + measured with oxygen sensor plug disconnected.
All measured in front of catalytic converter.

perform the tests described above and the procedure for this will be found in the next section.

Idle adjustment is performed on a sleeve screw found at the front of the twin throttle housing.

FUEL SUPPLY
Early models have one fuel delivery pump, located on anti- vibration mountings, just in front of the rear mounted fuel tank. Between the tank and pump is a small drum-shaped fuel silencer, which is a sealed unit. Its purpose is to eliminate the noise of fuel travelling from the tank. If it leaks it must be replaced. The pump itself is a caged roller type, where the whole electrical unit is fully immersed in fuel. Because there is no air inside the unit there is no risk of fire. On pre-1981 models, there is no one-way

The post-1981 injector, with screw-in metal fitting.

valve on the outlet from the pump. This valve should be retrofitted to reduce hot-start problems on the early models. The valve can be taken out and cleaned if necessary.

Initial delivery fuel pump, located on fuel tank.

The fuel filter on Series 2 924 Turbo is behind the engine splash wall. Note the good practice of writing the change date on the filter.

The fuel tank sender, under the rear luggage area.

Certain later models have an initial delivery pump, fitted to the base of the fuel tank. The fuel filter should be replaced every 30,000 miles or sooner if the filter history is unknown or the fuel considered dirty.

If the engine is not getting enough fuel or none at all, the electrical system can be used for diagnosis, but with caution. The ignition can be switched on without running the engine to measure fuel flow into a container. Pull the plug on the alternator, to avoid the possibility of burn-ing out its diodes. If there is a problem with fuel delivery, first check that the fuel pump is working by listening for its 'motor' noise, with the ignition on (put your ear close to it!). If it is not working, check that there is approximately 12 volts at its connections.

The output of the pump can be checked by detaching the fuel return line from the fuel metering unit and holding it over a 1 litre (1 US qt) measuring jar. The flexible intake ducting over the metering unit will have to be removed to do this. Be careful not to kink the fuel lines.

On pre-1979 models the fuel pump can be activated by lifting the flow sensor plate. On later models locate the fuel pump relay near the fuse panel. The relays are located in the passenger footwell and the fuel pump relay is the second in from the left on the top row. Locate terminals 30 and 87 on the board and insert jumper lead between them, bridged by an 8 amp fuse. The fuse is very important in case there is a short somewhere else in the circuit. The jumper lead will also tell you whether the relay itself is faulty. Switch on the ignition only (not activating the starter) and time thirty seconds and switch off again. The return line should have filled the jar with at least 750 cc. If it is less, then the pump, the accumulator or the filter are at fault.

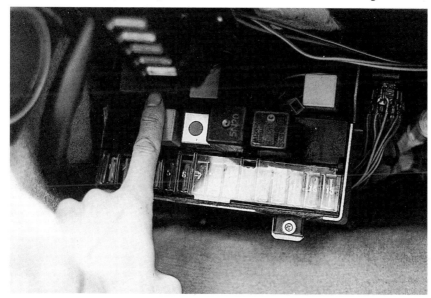

The relay panel of earlier models was in the left-hand footwell. Fuel pump relay is indicated.

At the start of the 1985 model year the relays and fuses moved to the old battery position, behind the engine splash wall.

If the jumper lead fuse blew when in the circuit, it may prove the pump is taking too much current and is faulty (necessitating renewal). If the fuel volume into the jar is short or the pump sounds erratic, measure the current taken by placing an ammeter in series with one of the pump connections. If the pump is fine it should be taking about 6.5 amps, but no more than 8.5 amps. If it is nearer the higher figure, maybe the filter needs replacing.

INJECTORS

924 injectors are a push fit into bushes on the inlet manifold. They are working in an area of low pressure, so they tend to be pulled into the manifold rather than blown out. If the bushes are cracked or broken they should be replaced. The bushes should be 'wetted' with fuel before assembly to the manifold or fitting the injector.

If the engine is running roughly it can mean that a cylinder is not getting sufficient fuel, assuming the spark plugs are in good condition and correctly gapped. To check an injector, stop the engine and pull the suspect injector out of its mounting bush in the cylinder head. Plug the resulting hole in the bush using a cork or similar (but remember you will want to get it out again). Place the injector into a glass jar. Taking care not to touch any of the moving engine parts, ask a friend to start the engine. Remember that the fuel can be explosively flammable. Observe the injector spray. If it is not a symmetrical cone, then the injector should be replaced. When the engine is switched off the spray should stop, with no dribble. If there is dribbling this could cause starting problems. Check the output of each injector in turn for a given time, say thirty seconds, the delivery of each should be approximately the same.

The special injector cleaning compounds that are retailed as fuel additives will only clean away mild gumming, so don't expect too much

of them. Injectors are relatively cheap and replacement can produce a significant improvement in starting performance and smoothness on an older car. The retightening torque for an injector to its feed line is 25 Nm (18 lb ft).

CHECKING THE AIR SENSOR PLATE

Run the engine for a few minutes to build up a residual pressure in the fuel lines. Remove the rubber ducting that joins the air filter housing. There should be an even gap of 0.1 mm (0.004 in) all around the plate, relative to the bore. The plate's upper edge should be level with, or no more than 0.5 mm (0.020 in) below the start of the venturi, when the residual pressure is removed. If an adjustment is necessary, the wire bracket beneath the plate can be bent, but it is strongly recommended this is done by a specialist. The central nut should be refitted with thread locking adhesive, if removed. Be very careful not to damage the surface of the venturi.

THERMO-TIME SWITCH

The jumper wire mentioned earlier can be used to test the operation of this unit, located on the engine block. By removing the cold start valve and directing it into a suitable container, the time can be measured that the valve remains open after the engine begins to turn over. On a reasonably cold engine, it should close within 3-10 seconds and not dribble at all. The thermo-switch should be replaced if there is no fuel spray or if it dribbles.

EMISSIONS EQUIPMENT

Until the end of the 1979 model year US models were fitted with exhaust gas recirculation (EGR) for emissions control. This complicated system reduces the levels of the oxides of nitrogen (NOx) in the exhaust by injecting inert gas into the combustion chambers. The inert gas used is the exhaust gas, this being injected in small quantities downstream of the throttle butterflies. This slows the combustion process and reduces the likelihood of NOx forming. The EGR system results in a poorer fuel consumption, is more expensive to manufacture and most importantly uses valuable engine power to drive its pump.

The EGR system was superseded in 1980 by the Lambda system, which uses an oxygen sensor fitted to the exhaust manifold to detect the level of oxygen in the burned gases. When the oxygen level in the system is detected as low, the sensor estimates the amount by which the mixture is too rich for the prevailing engine loading. This information is passed to an electronic control unit located under the steering column. A frequency valve then adjusts the fuel/air ratio to restore the mixture to a satisfactory level for the given load. Similarly, when the sensor indicates an over- lean mixture the control unit increases the fuel supply. Two microswitches ensure a suitably rich mixture for idle and full load (above 3500 rpm).

Other emissions control equipment has been variously used on those 924 models destined for the US (including California), Canada and Japan. These include evaporative emission control (EEC) using a charcoal canister, air injection and catalytic converters. For more information on these, the reader is directed to the Haynes Owners Workshop Manual on the 924.

924 SYSTEM TROUBLE-SHOOTING TABLE

Before tearing the hardware apart, check there is fuel in the tank, the battery is properly connected and so on. Sometimes there is an easy answer to the problem! It is assumed also that the engine and its ignition system are fully serviceable. This is only a simple guide and not intended to be exhaustive. Where feasible the diagnosis methods used have been described above.

Symptom: Poor Starting

Fault	Need to check
Poor fuel pump output.	750 cc output in 30 secs from fuel feed to distributor.
Dirty or blocked lines/injectors/fuel filter.	Check and clean all items/no kinks in lines.
Leaks in air system.	Check all unions for tightness, splits, etc.
Cold start valve does not work.	Remove valve and watch spray 'cone' for 3-10 seconds.
Thermo-time switch does not work.	Pull plug to cold start valve. Fit test light to plug from switch. Start engine and light should go off in 3-10 seconds if engine temp less than 40 °C.
Auxiliary air valve does not work.	Check hoses for kinks, use mirror to look at valve, check operation.
Control pressure too low.	Use pressure gauge. Regulator may be defective.
Sensor plate/metering piston faulty.	Smooth movement of plate and piston upwards. Piston falls slowly when plate released suddenly. Sticky movement means plate position should be adjusted or clean/replace piston.

PORSCHE 924

Symptom: Will Not Start When Hot

Control/system pressure low.	Test for leaks.
Faulty thermo-time switch.	Floods engine when hot. Test as above, if engine temp over 40°C and light on, replace switch.
Leaking injectors/cold start valve	Check for dribbles; should be none when system pressurised. Check also one way valve fitted after fuel pump if pre- '81 model.

Symptom: High Fuel Consumption

Leaking fuel injectors/cold start valve.	Check as above.
Control pressure low.	Check with gauge.
Idle screw adjusted incorrectly.	Take to specialist for adjustment using CO meter.
Sticking metering piston/sensor plate.	Seek specialist advice.

Symptom: Uneven Running

Faulty fuel pump.	Check voltage of pump. If less than 11.5 V check supply and connections. If 11.5 V or higher, replace pump (no whirring noise when ignition on).
Faulty injectors.	Remove and check cone spray. Check opening at correct system pressure.
Idle mixture incorrect.	Use CO meter or adjust as in text.
Faulty air intake ducting.	Check all ducting and connections.

114

PART 2

OUTLINE OF THE 944 SYSTEM

The 944 uses the mechanically simpler but all-electronically controlled Bosch L-Jetronic system. This works as an integrated unit with the Bosch Digital Engine Electronics (DEE) or Motronic system which also controls the engine's ignition. The system ensures that the mixture is held within much closer tolerances than is possible with the K-Jetronic system. The control also suits the higher compression ratio of the 2.5-litre engine and enables better performance and fuel consumption to be achieved.

Although the sensor inputs are found on the K-Jetronic system, the control comes from a microprocessor chip (PROM) on which is stored the fuel injection 'map' data. These data principally relate information on engine rpm, load and throttle position. The easiest way to consider this is to think of a graph with three axes, where any point can be defined by x, y, z co-ordinates. This permits the data at any point to be stored digitally. The engine 'map', or the envelope on the graph that relates the rpm, load and throttle position, is determined during the car's development as offering the best compromise of performance, fuel consumption and so on. The map information is defined by digitising the points (256 of them) that form its envelope and these data are placed on the chip at the factory. The

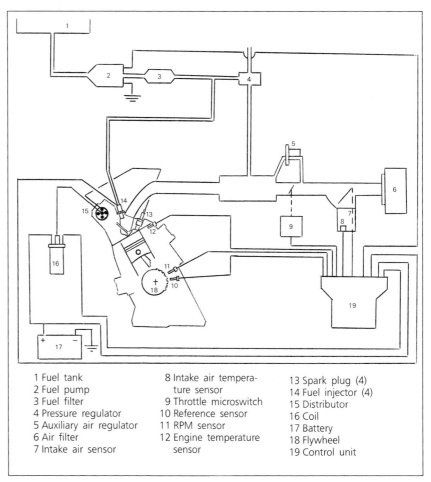

1 Fuel tank	8 Intake air tempera-	13 Spark plug (4)
2 Fuel pump	ture sensor	14 Fuel injector (4)
3 Fuel filter	9 Throttle microswitch	15 Distributor
4 Pressure regulator	10 Reference sensor	16 Coil
5 Auxiliary air regulator	11 RPM sensor	17 Battery
6 Air filter	12 Engine temperature	18 Flywheel
7 Intake air sensor	sensor	19 Control unit

data can only be changed by replacing the chip. The engine map is not something to be played with, unless there is full access to the development data that went into the origi-

The integrated L-Jetronic and Motronic systems of the 944.

The ducting from the air sensor housing and the throttle housing.

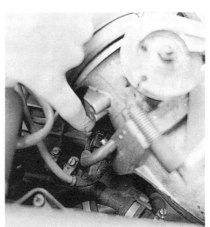

The throttle switch on the single throttle butterfly.

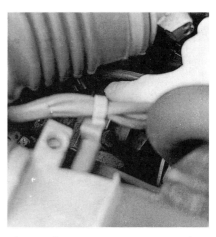

The engine temperature sensor is located under the flexible ducting.

nal and a thorough knowledge is possessed of digital engine electronics. Unskilled reprogramming can lead to reduced engine reliability, heavy fuel consumption and worse.

Cold-start fuel is metered directly by the injectors and is dependent on engine temperature and rpm.

The injection is interrupted on the over-run, depending on the engine temperature. This occurs above 1,900 rpm with a cold engine, but above 1,600 rpm with the engine warm. The injection continues when the revs drop 400 below these figures. Over-revving is also controlled by the injectors with cut-off being made above 6,500 rpm. Throttle response is also improved by full-load enrichment variable with engine temperature.

The fuel system components function in much the same way as with the K-Jetronic equipment and you may find it useful to read through

the preceding section on that system. Where sensors provide data directly to bi-metallic actuators in the K-Jetronic system, the L-Jetronic passes the information to the chip for comparison of the input to the reference or 'ideal' information of the engine map. The output then provides more sensitive control of the actuators, etc in the fuel system. The air being drawn into the engine is still monitored by the air sensor plate, where an intake air temperature sensor is also located. There is only a single throttle butterfly. Fuel passes from the tank to pump and filter to a fuel distribution tube located above the four injectors. Throttle position is monitored by a throttle switch. The system pressure is maintained by a regulator, which also provides cold start enrichment and there is none of the complicated mechanical fuel distributor valving of the K-Jetronic arrangement. The mixture does not rely on a control pressure circuit but on the comparison of sensor inputs with the digitised map.

The bottom line is that this is not a system to mess with unless you really know what you are doing. Indeed, it is actually quite difficult to

tamper with it seriously because it is controlled electronically.

ADJUSTING THE IDLE SPEED
Before altering the idle adjustment screw, check that the fuel delivery is satisfactory (using exactly the same method as with the K-Jetronic) and the engine ignition and spark plugs are working normally.

This adjustment should be done with a CO tester, so that the mixture can be set correctly at the same time. The warning relating to mixture adjustment given in the 924 section is repeated here. Adjusting the mixture is a fine balance of several variables and must only be performed with trained use of a sensitive CO meter. In the USA the mixture is the key adjustment for controlling emissions and should only be performed by a specialist.

The DEE alters the timing in the idle speed range also, so it is important to have the idle set correctly. The engine oil temperature should be 80°C, or fully warmed up. A separate tachometer will be necessary for accurate setting of idle speed to CO level. Alternatively, use a strobe timing light on the flywheel reference

Idle adjustment screw on the throttle housing.

'dot' to establish accurately the correct idle speed. The standard in-car rev counters have been known to be up to 10 per cent in error on some 924/944 models.

The temperature sensor in the throttle housing/air distributor should be unscrewed and placed over the splash wall, behind the engine. The leads to it should be left connected. This is so that the sensor will be in fresh ambient air and not influenced by the engine warming up. An M14 x 1.5 plug should be fitted in the opening left in the housing.

The engine should not be loaded whilst at idle, so turn off lights, fans, air conditioning and other power users. On models fitted with a catalytic converter, connect the CO meter to the union ahead of the converter canister, using an exhaust gas test line. The plug for the oxygen sensor should also be detached during measurement with a CO meter. When refitting the cap nut at the converter union (torque 30 Nm,

22 lb ft), coat the nut with a high temperature molybdenum disulphide grease for easy removal next time.

The idle adjustment screw is located on the throttle housing, on the side closest to the air filter. The vertically-positioned screw is located inside a flange to prevent accidental movement. The mixture control screw is located on the air sensor housing. It is covered by a plastic cap and is on the throttle housing side of the casting.

Right: Mixture adjustment on the air sensor plate housing. Note also the plug to the inlet air temperature sensor.

Set the idle first, to the speed specified in the data table at the end of this section.

If the engine has been rebuilt and the correct setting of the mixture screw is not known, a coarse adjustment can be obtained by starting the engine and letting it idle until warm. Weaken the mixture (turn screw counter-clockwise) until the engine just falters, then back off the screw clockwise (richen) about a quarter turn until the engine runs smoothly. Check the idle speed again and reset if necessary. The mixture/idle speed should then be set accurately using the CO meter. This fine adjustment is essential to prevent the effects of an incorrect mixture on the engine and to meet emissions laws in certain countries.

FUEL SUPPLY
The fuel pressure should be checked using a pressure gauge. The gauge described in the K-Jetronic section can be used. The factory tester is tool number P378. The pipe end with the external thread should be blocked off and the M12 internally threaded nut on the other pipe connected to the

union on the end of the fuel distribution pipe, above the injectors. Ensure the sealing ball does not fall out when the capped nut is removed from the end of the pipe. The fuel pump relay will be found in the relay box. The relay should be pulled out

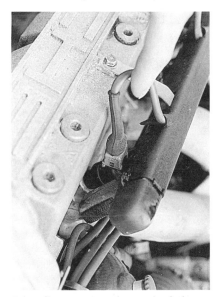

Snap-fit cover on the end of the fuel distribution pipe protects pressure testing nut. The connector fits directly to the fuel injector.

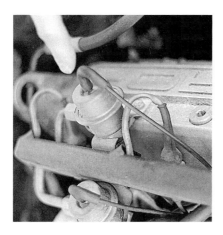

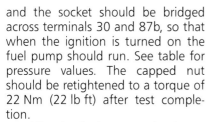

The fuel pressure regulator on this 1983 944 is on the camshaft housing side of the distribution pipe. On the other side is the diaphragm damper.

A view of the 944's rear underside, showing the initial delivery and main fuel pumps.

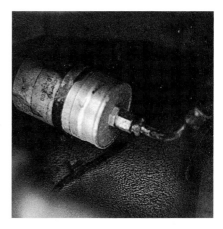

The 944 fuel filter is on the delivery side of the main fuel pump and is fitted to the underbody, just ahead of the right hand drive shaft.

and the socket should be bridged across terminals 30 and 87b, so that when the ignition is turned on the fuel pump should run. See table for pressure values. The capped nut should be retightened to a torque of 22 Nm (22 lb ft) after test completion.

Whilst the fuel pump relay is out and terminals 30 and 87b are bridged, the fuel delivery can be checked. Unscrew the return hose on the pressure regulator, located at the rear of the fuel distributor pipe, on the side of the cam cover. The return pipe comes out at the base of the unit. Find a suitable container that will hold about a litre (1 US qt) and place it so that returned fuel fills the container. Let the fuel fill the container for 30 seconds; see table for data. If there is less than the necessary volume the fuel pump could be faulty or the fuel filter may need changing. The fuel filter is located next to the fuel pump, at the rear of the car. The fuel feed line should be clamped to prevent fuel spillage. The filter is a canister with a fuel line

entering at one end and another line exiting from the other. The nuts holding the lines are locked against the filter body and this should be gripped with another spanner, whilst the nuts are loosened. The new filter has a

'direction of flow' arrow indicating which way it fits. After fitting, remove the clamp and run the engine to check for leaks from the filter connections and the adjacent fuel lines.

L-JETRONIC DATA

TEST	SPECIFICATION
Fuel pump delivery rate.	At least 850 cc (52 cu in) per 30 seconds.
Fuel pressure, engine stopped:	
with fuel pump bridged -	2.5 +/-0.2 bar (37 +/- 3 psi)
at idle speed -	approx. 2 bar (29 psi)
Idle speed (rpm):	
Europe -	800 +/-50
USA/Canada/Japan -	900 +/-50
Australia/Sweden -	800 +/-50
	(For auto transmission or power steering cars, adjust to top limit).
CO level (%):	
Europe	0.5 to 1.0
USA/Canada/Japan	0.6 +/-0.2
Australia/Sweden	0.5 to 1.0

CHAPTER 7

IGNITION SYSTEMS

There was a step change in the electronic technology between the original 2-litre 924 and the 1980 Carrera GT. The digital technology introduced on the GT, that replaced the earlier inductive ignition fitted to the 924 and early 924 Turbos, was subsequently developed and fitted to the Series 2 924 Turbo and all the later 944 types. Both systems were integrated with the starting and fuel delivery systems, but it was the method of control which developed dramatically. I will not spend any time here discussing the coil ignition system fitted to the early European models as the principles and fault-finding techniques have been amply described in other books.

Before getting into the practical discussion, I must mention safety. The method of operation of transistorised ignition means that very high levels of voltage and current are being used. Contact with the current-carrying parts of both the inductive and digital system, when the engine is running can be lethal. Before physical contact with any part of the ignition system, you must switch off the engine and disconnect the battery.

PART 1

924 IGNITION SYSTEM

There was a time not so long ago when a car with transistor ignition was considered very advanced. Unlike the earlier magneto or points-controlled coil methods, the transistorised method had the ability to deliver a fat spark to the plugs at all engine speeds. The method also permitted a higher voltage than the coil system and this factor permitted a larger plug gap. As a result torque was improved, potentially without any reduction of fuel consumption.

The system on all US and post 1980 European 2-litre 924 models is an inductive ignition circuit. The system requires no points. The main components are the transistor ignition control unit, an ignition coil and a distributor. It is the control unit which makes the points redundant, the transistor acting as the switch. The transistor uses small switching currents in a separate gate circuit to give on/off control over the large currents of the ignition circuit.

The transistor has three terminals: the emitter, which is connected to earth; the collector, which picks up a 12 volt potential from the coil primary lead; and the base, which turns the current on and off. The emitter terminal is terminal 5 on the ignition control unit. The collector is terminal 6 (connected to terminal 1 on the coil). The base is either terminal 1 or 2. The rev counter is, incidentally, taken off terminal 3 on the control unit.

Power is supplied to the ignition circuit through the ignition lock and switched by the transistor to terminal 15 of the coil. The amount of current passing is generally 4 amps. The flow is maintained 'on' by the trigger circuit, by keeping 0.1 amp applied to the base terminal.

When the distributor rotor turns, one of the four points on the rotor will pass over the base terminal contact in the distributor body. This interrupts the power flow and the trigger circuit goes to 'off'. A surge of current then leaves the coil's central HT terminal, passes through the distributor, the rotor and out to the appropriate spark plug. The spark occurs at the plug gap as the current surge arcs to the earth outer body of the plug. The advantage of the transistor switching is its capacity for very rapid build up and discharge, unlike the traditional system controlled by mechanical points, at a rate far greater than the engine needs sparks.

Transistorised ignition was fitted to the European 924 from the 1980 model year.

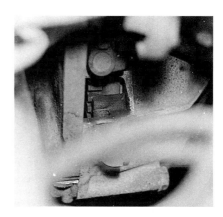

TROUBLE-SHOOTING

A very useful piece of equipment for troubleshooting electrical bugs is a hand-held multimeter which can read currents, voltages and resistances. Knowledge of the required values can considerably shorten the time taken to identify a fault. The instrument should come with all the necessary needle probes and small clips for attaching to all types of terminals.

If there is a problem with the car, which you think may be in the ignition circuit, do some basic checks first. Ensure the battery is fully charged and there is fuel in the tank! Follow the fuel system troubleshooting guide as well if it is not clear what the fault is. Assuming a component is faulty can be an unnecessarily expensive way of solving the problem.

Spark plug access to the 2-litre engine is not easy.

CHECKING THE IGNITION TIMING

If you are not familiar with this procedure as a result of working with other engines, then the advice is check only but do not alter the timing. With this guide you should be able to identify the problem, which will save a specialist's time to remedy the fault.

Right: *Plug on the left-hand wing, which can be linked together to bypass the electronic idle stabiliser fitted to US models.*

The engine should be at normal operating temperature, with the oil temperature at 80–90°C. On European versions the vacuum hose to the advance/retard unit in the distributor should be disconnected, but on US/Japanese versions leave them connected. A remote tachometer connected as directed by its manufacturer will give a more accurate reading of idle rpm than the unit in the car. A strobe timing light is used to observe the position of the timing mark on the flywheel against the reference edge at idle speed (on most models 950 +/- 50 rpm, but see Chapter 6). If the idle speed, measured on the tachometer, is not correct then adjust this before checking the timing. Point the beam of the strobe at the open slot in the bellhousing (at the upper left side, to the rear of the engine). Check the specification table for your model for the correct timing mark, which should align with the reference mark at the correct idle speed. If it does not appear, or is not right, loosen the distributor and rotate it carefully until alignment is achieved. The tightening torque of the distributor clamp nut is 20–22 Nm (14–16 lbft).

For the European version the timing should be 10 degrees before Top Dead Centre (TDC) without the vacuum hose being attached. When set, the '+10' aligns with the reference mark at the idle speed. For US/Japanese models, do not disconnect the vacuum hose. Early US models (pre-1977½ model year) were set to 10 degrees after TDC, at which position a '-' appears aligned with the mark. US models from then onwards to the end of the 1979 model year used 3 degrees after TDC, or '-3' aligned with the reference mark. From the 1980 model year, US models were set to exact TDC, with a '0' appearing aligned with the mark. Check your model data to confirm the correct setting.

If the timing is altered at idle, professional diagnostic equipment should be used to check the high speed timing.

USA MODEL DIFFERENCES

From the 1981 model year the 924 ignition system was fitted with a Hall transmitter (a magnetic sensor) and idle speed stabiliser. An electronic idle stabiliser (EIS) was fitted on the engine compartment wall of the left wheel arch. If the ignition system is giving problems, the EIS can be taken out of the circuit by pulling off its leads and directly connecting them.

PRE-1981 924 TURBO

The timing on all but the UK models was 20 degrees before TDC, measured at 2000 +/-50rpm. For the UK, the timing was 9 degrees before TDC at 950rpm or 25 degrees before TDC at 2000rpm. The necessary marks will be found on the flywheel.

PART 2

DIGITAL ENGINE ELECTRONICS

It was the 924 Carrera GT that featured the new digital, rather than analogue, electronic ignition. It was carried over to the Series 2 924 Turbo and was subsequently installed from the start of 944 production, being given the more marketable title of Motronic ignition. The principles have remained the same up to the current models, although extensive development of the original concept has taken place.

Series 2 924 Turbo and Carrera GT. Digital Electronic Ignition (DEE) diagram.

I have described briefly the theory of the Digital Engine Electronics (DEE) principle in Chapter 6. The main aspects to remember are that the data used to control the ignition and fuel system are engine speed and intake vacuum, but supplemented by data on charge air temperature and throttle position. These are compared with preprogrammed optimum settings for any given engine loading that are stored in the electronic control unit's microprocessor. The output is continuously varied fuel delivery and ignition timing to give optimum performance, whilst achieving acceptable fuel consumption and exhaust emissions.

The major components of the DEE are shown on the accompanying dia-

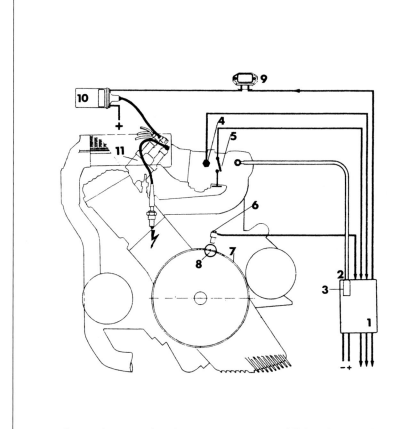

1	Electronic control unit	7	Additional gear ring
2	Pressure line	8	Reference mark
3	Pressure sensor	9	TCI control unit
4	Temperature sensor	10	Ignition coil
5	Throttle switch	11	High voltage distributor
6	Speed reference mark sensor		

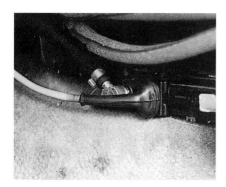

The electronic control unit is located in front of the centre console on the Series 2 924 Turbo. The farthest plug is the pressure sensor, the middle plug is the pulse transmitter and nearest is the multi-pin connector.

The electronic control unit on the 944 is under the dash panel on the driver's side.

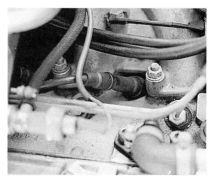

The spark plugs of the 924 Turbo are much easier to remove than those of the 924.

gram. The electronic control unit is located under the central console, below the heater on the 924 models. On its left-hand side it has a hose connection for the pressure sensor and a large flat multi-pin electrical connector. On the 944 it is located under the dash panel, next to the steering column.

The throttle switch and temperature sensor are fitted to the front of the throttle housing. The intake vacuum is measured from a threaded connection to the rear of the air distributor (the casting with the 'Porsche' lettering on it). The speed reference sensor uses an additional gear-like rim on the flywheel to measure rpm. The sensor is mounted on the top of the bell-housing directly behind the area on the block that has the engine number stamped on it. Access to it is not easy! The extra gear form profile on the flywheel rim has 100 'teeth'. One of these is the reference mark and is fitted with a soft iron insert. The sensor counts the number of teeth and because it records an 'on' and 'off' pulse for each tooth, it sends 200 changes of voltage pulse per engine

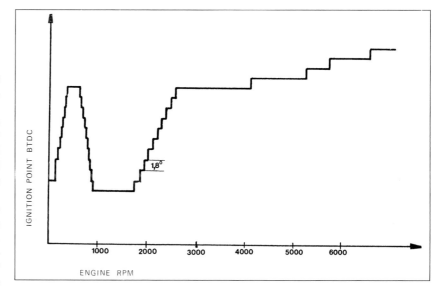

DEE ignition characteristic at full load.

revolution, or one every 1.8 degrees of crankshaft revolution. The ignition timing can then be varied in steps of 1.8 degrees of crankshaft rotation. The reference mark tooth, because of its insert, sends two, higher voltage pulses than the other teeth, from which the exact ignition timing angle is calculated by the processor. The processor calculates the engine speed from the number of reference pulses per time unit.

The distributor is sensorless and only distributes high voltage to each spark plug.

TROUBLE-SHOOTING DEE

Fault finding for the enthusiast is restricted to the power supply for the DEE and the fuel pump. Diagnostic work with the DEE requires an oscilloscope to do correctly and should be left to a specialist. If in doubt, don't touch anything!

There are some 'golden rules' to be

observed when working with integrated circuit equipment.

1) Never start the engine without the battery connected.

2) Incorrect connection of the battery can destroy the control unit.

3) Never start the engine with a rapid charger. Using jump leads from another 12 volt battery is OK.

4) Always disconnect the battery before charging.

5) Do not disconnect the battery whilst the engine is running.

6) Never connect or disconnect the flat multi-pin plug to the control unit whilst the engine is running.

7) Ensure the earth lead between the engine and body is connected before starting the engine (for instance after engine-out work). Failure to do this will destroy the control unit.

8) Before doing any electric welding on the car, disconnect the multi-pin plug to the control unit.

9) When doing a compression test pull off the fuel pump relay.

Given that the control unit takes on 'black box' status for the enthusiast, the objective here has been to give a basic understanding of the system components. The DEE system is very reliable, and faults, when they occur, can be fairly simple. When component failure is found, replacement is the only action and that is where it can get expensive. Careful handling of the system can prevent accidental damage.

Always check electrical plug and earth connections, throughout the system first, whether the problem is non-starting, poor idling, misfiring or insufficient power. This is a list of connectors that can be checked.

1) There are two earths to the engine block, next to the pulse transmitters at the rear of the engine, check these for cleanliness and good contact.

2) Check also the earth between the engine and the body behind and to

Left: *Series 2 924 Turbo ignition control unit, with large heat sink attached.*

Below: *Top view of the ignition coil on the Series 2 924 Turbo.*

Bottom: *The fitting on the 944 bellhousing for the speed and reference sensors. Note the 'D' and 'B' markings.*

the right of the fuel system distribution tube.

3) Check the plug connections for tight fit, bent plug sleeves and corrosion. To remove the multi-pin plug on the 944, push the catch to the right and pull the plug out forwards.

4) Check the plug connectors for the speed and (on the 944) reference mark transmitters. On the 944, the two sensors are mounted beside each other. The speed sensor lead is marked 'DG' and the reference mark sensor lead marked 'BG'. The position of each sensor is indicated by a 'B' and a 'D' marked on the clutch housing next to each fitting. These sensors work on a magnetic principle, so

be careful not to let any ferrous parts attach themselves to the sensor body. Do not overtighten the sensor into the clutch housing. The torque

PORSCHE 944

Note that the leads are marked 'DG' for the speed sensor and 'BG' for the reference sensor.

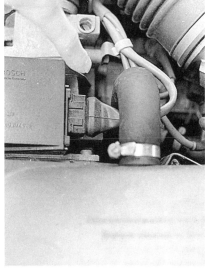

The plug connector for the air flow sensor on a 944.

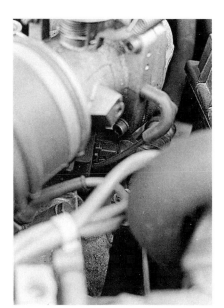

Throttle switch and engine temperature sensor are both under the throttle housing on the 944.

recommended is 8 Nm (5.9 lb ft).
5) Check the plug connector for the air flow sensor, on the rear of the air sensor plate housing.
6) Check the plugs for the throttle switch and the engine temperature sensor. On the 944 the throttle switch is located on the throttle housing casting, close to the flexible black ducting that leads from the air sensor housing. The engine temperature switch is under the same flexible ducting.
7) Check the plug connections to the fuel injectors.

8) Check the socket for the fuel pump relay.
9) Check the 9-pin connector mounted above the brake servo (booster) unit.

COMPONENT TESTING
If you have access to a multimeter, several sensors can be tested for function.
The airflow sensor switch can be checked during trouble-shooting for most non-starting or uneven running problems. Pull back its sleeve, leaving the plug connected. Measure the vol-

tage across its terminal 9 and earth, with the ignition on. It should read more than 8 volts. Remove the air filter so that the air sensor plate can be moved by hand. With the voltmeter now across terminal 7 and earth, between 150 and 250 millivolts should be seen with the ignition on. When the sensor plate is

Below: *Plug numbering on the 944. The two small connectors from the DEE plug go to the speed sensor (A) and the altitude box (B, USA only).*

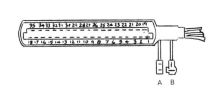

D E E CONTROL UNIT PLUG

THROTTLE SWITCH PLUG

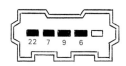

AIRFLOW SENSOR PLUG

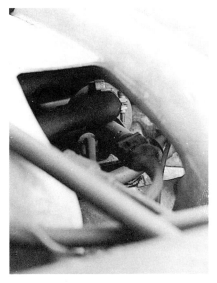

Throttle by-pass valve on the 944.

moved to the full throttle position the voltage rises above 8 volts.

To check the intake air temperature sensor, turn the ignition off and pull off the intake sensor plug. The resistance measured across the sensor's terminals 6 and 22 should be 1.45 to 3.3 kOhms, with the ambient air temperature between 15 and 30°C.

Left top: *A little time spent considering how it all fits together can save a nightmare later on.*

Left bottom: *The starter motor is fitted to the rear of the bellhousing on the 944, underneath the torque tube; access can be made only from below.*

The engine temperature switch should be checked if the engine will not start, if there is poor idling or high fuel consumption. Its location is described in the last section. The resistance between terminal 13 on the disconnected DEE plug and earth should again be 1.45 to 3.3 kOhms, with the engine cold and the air tem-perature as above. If these values are not met, test the sensor itself and replace if necessary.

The throttle switch location is also described previously. It can be the cause of poor pick-up, low power or high fuel consumption. The resistance between the DEE plug terminal 2 and earth should be zero with the throttle closed and infinity with it open. Switching should occur within 1 degree of the throttle closed position. The resistance between terminal 3 and earth is the opposite, namely infinity with the throttle closed and zero with it open. The switching here should occur just before the fully open position. Again, if these values are not met, test the switch by connecting the resistance meter to terminal 18 (earth) and 1 and 2 in turn.

The throttle switch position can adjusted on the 944 by loosening its mounting screws, holding the throttle butterfly fully closed and turning the switch until a stop is felt. Do not move the butterfly. The switch should be tightened at this stop position.

Non-starting or poor idling could also suggest a faulty throttle by-pass valve. A simple method of checking its operation is to let the engine get fully warmed and then pinch the flexible air hose that leads to or from the valve. The engine idle rpm should only drop a fraction, because the valve should already be closed. The resistance of the valve should be 30 to 65 Ohms on pre-August 1982 models and 20 to 55 Ohms on later models. The valve should receive battery voltage.

OTHER ELECTRICAL SYSTEM COMPONENTS
I have assumed that the area of most interest will be the ignition system, so I have not discussed the starting circuitry and other electrical equipment here. When doing any diagnostic work on any parts in the electrical system, don't race straight in and tear everything out! Just look at the connections and note down where they all go. A good idea is to use masking tape to make labels for each wire, lead or hose and record on these where they connect before removal. A little time spent considering how it all goes together, can save a nightmare later on.

CHAPTER 8
CLUTCH TRANSMISSION AND SUSPENSION

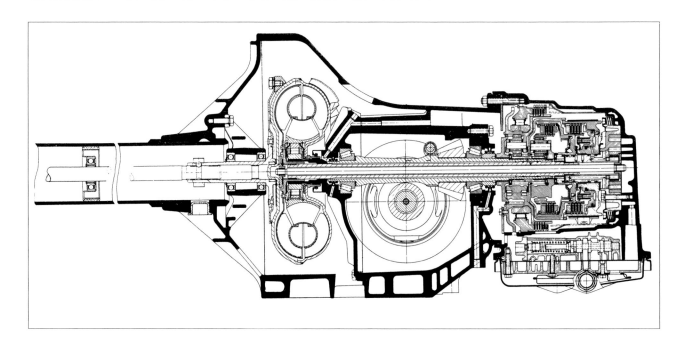

PART 1

CLUTCH

It is quite possible to replace the clutch on all models, with the engine still in the car. However, all the work is beneath the car and it is necessary to raise the car safely to a satisfactory working height, that will allow access to the front and rear ends of the transmission. Putting the car up on axle stands is not really high enough and a professional lift is best for the job. The clutch is removed by sliding the gearbox, torque tube assembly and bellhousing backwards by about 100mm (4 ins) to get access from the front of the bellhousing to the clutch. Great care is necessary during the work to ensure the torque tube is not allowed to take any bending loads.

This skeleton view shows the major components of the transmission. The clutch and gearbox are linked by a rigid tube containing the propeller shaft.

Because most who read this will not contemplate changing the clutch themselves, I will concentrate on fault-finding and inspection.

As always, the advice is: leave it to a specialist if you are unsure of what to do. The full descriptions of the stripdowns are given in the Haynes Owners Workshop Manuals on the 924 (Bk No 397) and 944 (Bk No 1027 US).

Don't forget safety. Don't work under a car that is supported solely by the tyre change jack. Make sure it is stable on axle stands and always have someone else nearby, when you are working underneath.

CLUTCH INSPECTION
The clutch used on both the manual 924 and 944 is the single, dry plate diaphragm type located in the bellhousing bolted to the rear of the engine block. On the 924 it is cable

944 clutch assembly, with the friction plate uppermost.

operated. The 924 Turbo and 944 use hydraulic operation, with the clutch pedal operating the piston of a master cylinder located inside the engine compartment. A hydraulic line links the master cylinder to a slave cylinder or actuator mounted at the base of the bellhousing. The actuator operates the clutch release bearing in the same way as the purely

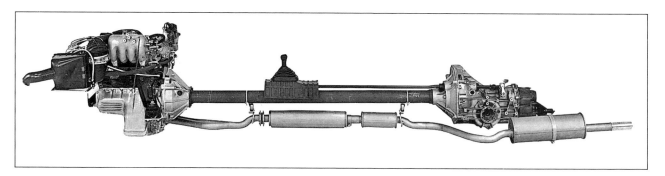

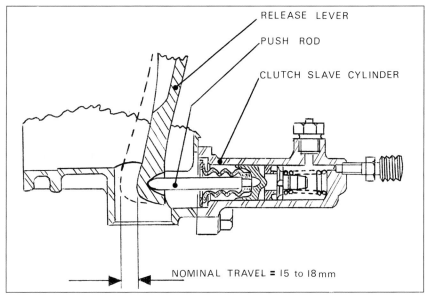

RELEASE LEVER

PUSH ROD

CLUTCH SLAVE CYLINDER

NOMINAL TRAVEL = 15 to 18mm

The clutch plumbing dismantled. Nearest the camera is the clutch master cylinder, with its reservoir. The twisted pipe leads to the slave cylinder in the bellhousing (over the starter motor, here).

Setting dimension for the mechanical operation of the 924 clutch.

mechanical linkage. The torque tube is attached to the bellhousing by four bolts and contains the propeller shaft linking the clutch to the rear-mounted gearbox.

The condition of the clutch can be inspected from under the car. The car must be securely lifted and supported to do this. A pair of vernier calipers will be useful to measure the key dimensions.

On all the 924 models, you have to remove the single cross-head screw that attaches the inspection cover to the clutch bellhousing. Check the wear of the friction material and compare the thickness with the specification. The 924 friction plate should be 10.1–10.5 mm (0.4–0.41 in) when new and minimum thickness, if the wear is completely even, is 8.5 mm (0.35 in). The 924 Turbo's friction plate thickness

new is 8.1 +/-0.3 mm (0.32 +/-0.012 in). The wear limit is 6.3 mm (0.25 in), for even wear. Vernier calipers should be used to measure these dimensions.

The maximum run-out or uneven wear allowed is 0.6 mm (0.024 in). The engine should be turned by hand, so that the wear can be observed all around the circumference of the disc. The engine can be turned over by hand, by putting a spanner onto the crankshaft pulley bolt. The job will be easier if the spark plugs are removed.

The 944 friction plate wear is gauged by measuring the position of the release bearing lever. This is observed by removing the cap in the bellhousing, just ahead of the slave cylinder. The distance from the front edge of the inspection hole to the front face of the release lever (located in the bellhousing and visible through the hole) should be 18 mm (0.7 in) when new, with a wear limit dimension of 34 mm (1.33 in). If the wear

The flexible cap in the bellhousing is easily removed to check the position of the release bearing lever.

is out of spec, the clutch must be replaced. Asymmetrical wear may have been indicated by a vibration, which would worsen with rpm. Such wear is also very bad for the torque shaft bearings and, if not attended to, will result in noisy rotation of the tube. A heavily worn clutch will slip such that rpm rise erratically whilst accelerating. On no account attempt to clean the friction lining with any oil based solvent. If the clutch has been removed it may be cleaned carefully with acetone or naphtha.

CLUTCH ADJUSTMENT

For the mechanically operated 924 clutch, adjustment must be performed from under the car, so follow the inspection procedure above first. There should be 20–25 mm (0.75–1.00 in) free play at the pedal and the dimension between the slot in the end of the clutch lever (which links the cable to the release bearing), and the lower edge of the cable adjuster bracket should be 138 +/–2 mm (5.43 +/–0.08 in). Use a screwdriver to push the release bearing into positive contact with the clutch diaphragm spring before measuring this latter dimension.

On the hydraulically operated clutch systems, the clutch play is self-adjusting. There should be about 3 mm (0.12 in) of free play at the clutch pedal for both 924 and 944. This can be adjusted by the lock nut on the master cylinder actuating piston, which is fitted to the clutch pedal.

Setting dimension for the hydraulically operated 924 Turbo and 944 clutch.

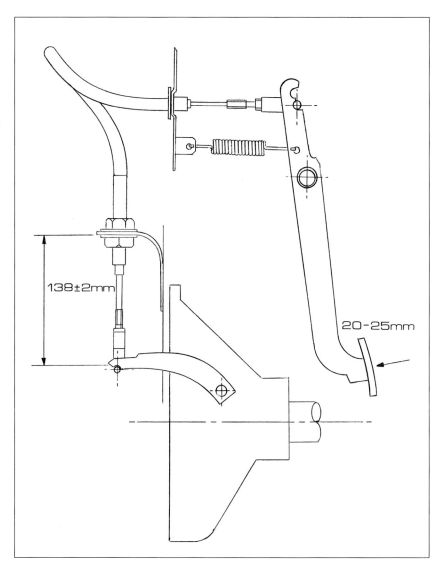

PART 2

TRANSMISSION

DRIVE SHAFTS

A whirring drive shaft is a frequently noticed problem with any 924 model with more than about 30,000 (careful) miles. It is not something to get really worried about unless the noise is really intrusive. It can be detected when sitting in the stationary car with the engine running. Leave the gearbox in neutral and press the clutch in and out. If the shaft bearings are worn, you will hear the shaft starting to spin as the clutch is released. The advice is to live with the noise, unless perfection is required or the shaft sounds really shot. Replacement of the bearings is a difficult task and the factory recommendation is to replace the whole torque tube assembly.

GEARBOXES

The gearbox has been a particularly active area of development for the 924 and subsequent 944. There have been several different types, together with variations of ratios within a given type. Because of the complexity of gearbox internal layout, no description will be given here of inspection or maintenance. Stripping gearboxes should only be performed by a specialist.

Note that the gear clusters on the types 088 and 016/8, 9 gearboxes are behind the rear axle line and that the 016Z,Y have their clusters ahead of the axle line. For competition, a lower polar moment of inertia will be achieved with the cluster weight ahead of the rear axle line. However, note that a limited slip differential was an option from 1982 models using the 016/8,9 types.

Full data on the different gearbox versions (including the automatic transmission) is given in Appendix 1.

P A R T 3

SUSPENSION AND BRAKES

FRONT AXLE

The front suspension on all the four-cylinder, water-cooled Porsches works on the MacPherson strut principle, with fully independent coil spring/damper units for each wheel.

All but one model have negative roll radius geometry designed into their front suspension. This is a safety feature which helps the driver should the car be heavily braked on unequal grip surfaces (or if one of the brake circuits fails, leaving only one front wheel with braking).

Consider the accompanying diagram. If an imaginary line was drawn from the top mounting point of the coil spring/damper, through the steering ball joint, it would touch the ground outside the contact point of the tyre. This geometry is termed negative roll radius or negative scrub. If the strut was positioned more vertically, the imaginary line would touch the ground inside the contact point; this would be positive roll radius. The effect of negative roll radius is to pull the car back into line when there is

a condition of unequal braking effort on the front wheels. Positive roll radius would tend to amplify the unstable condition, but can be preferred by competition drivers, who need to get the earliest feel for an unstable condition. The Carrera GT has positive roll radius for this reason.

FRONT ANTI-ROLL BAR

An anti-roll or stabiliser bar has always been available as an option on the front suspension of the 924, but in the 1981 model year one was

All the 924/944 series have Mac-Pherson strut independent front suspension.

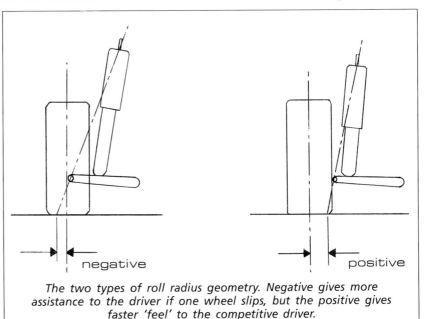

The two types of roll radius geometry. Negative gives more assistance to the driver if one wheel slips, but the positive gives faster 'feel' to the competitive driver.

133

fitted as standard. The details on sizes are given on the right. The standard front strut was made by VW, with Konis being available as an option for the 924 Turbo, the 944 and the Carrera GT (which also offered Bilsteins).

Type	Model year	Standard (mm)	Option (mm)
924	1977	–	20
924	1978	–	22
924	1979	–	23
924	1980	–	23
924	1981 to Sept 1981	21	23
924	1982 from Oct 1981	20	21.5
924 Turbo	all	23 (see below)	–
924 Carrera GT	all	23	–
944	all	20	21.5

Front anti-roll bar attaches to a fabricated lower control arm (944).

The 924 Turbo size given on the left was for Europe, Rest of World, with that size available as an option in US/Canada/Japan. The basic size for the US model from launch was 21mm. From 1981 the 23mm bar was only available in the US with a sports suspension pack which included Konis and a rear bar of 14mm.

FRONT SPRINGS

Coil springs come in different tolerance bands denoted by red, blue and green stripes. If the springs are removed, always refit pairs of springs with the same markings. If a single spring has to be changed, replace both because settling may have occurred with the remaining older spring. The table on the right is a listing of 924 Turbo/Carrera GT/944 spring ratings.

FRONT BRAKES

Don't work on the brakes unless you are trained to do so. Don't use an air line to clean around the brakes because the pads may contain asbestos; wipe away brake dust with a dampened cloth.

The 924 had 257mm (10.12 inch) solid front discs with a single-pot floating caliper. The 924 Turbo (and Carrera GT) received ventilated 282.5 mm (11.12 inch) discs for the first European, Rest of World models with the US/Canada/Japan models to the 1981 year keeping the basic 924 system (solid disc front/drum rear). From 1981, the US models were given the European spec brakes. This change to the US models was a major enhancement of the original

Right: *A single-pot floating front calliper on a 924 Turbo. The pads look OK and there's no evidence of fluid leakage.*

Group	Uncompressed length	Force at L = 251 mm	Colour Code
Spring 477 411 105Q (924 Turbo, 944)			
1	381mm	2727–2800N	1 blue
2	381mm	2800–2873N	2 blue
3	381mm	2873–2946	3 blue

Cars with air conditioning only use group 3 springs.

Group	Uncompressed length	Force at L = 251 mm	Colour Code
Spring 477 411 105G (Carrera GT)			
1	359mm	2502–2560N	1 red
2	359mm	2560–2629N	2 red
3	359mm	2629–2698N	3 red

Carrera GT ride height is 10mm lower than the 924 Turbo.

US Turbo spec.
Whereas the 924 caliper piston was 48 mm, the European Turbo went up to 54 mm (followed by the US cars for 1981).

The Carrera GT had special ducts fitted from the front spoiler to duct cooling air to the front discs. It also featured a major safety improvement in the use of a stepped, tandem

master cylinder (later also fitted to the 944).

To check the brake pad wear, the car should be placed securely on axle stands, with the rear wheels chocked. The front wheels should be removed. The minimum pad thickness for any of the 924/944 models is 2 mm (0.08 in). Replace the pads, if they are near or over this limit.

There is nothing complicated about changing the pads, if you are familiar with disc brake mechanics. Push each slave cylinder back into the caliper with a piece of wood (to avoid damage – but mind the seal!). Check before doing this that the reservoir will not overflow as the piston is moved back. Clean up the inside of the caliper with a brush and slide in the new pads, which should only be factory items. Replace the pads also if they have become contaminated with brake fluid, fuel or any oil-based substance. If the pads are taken out and then refitted make sure the same pad goes back into the same place in the same caliper.

Be very careful not to damage the

PORSCHE 924

disc, if an old pad needs to be dislodged, by light tapping. Inspect both sides of the disc for heavy grooving or ribbing. Such marking can promote a vibration whilst the car is in motion or promote a pull to one side. If marking is found, take advice from a specialist. The disc may need machining to restore a perfectly flat surface or even replacing.

Whilst the front wheels are removed, check the brake lines to the caliper for corrosion. Check also for evidence of leaks from the pipework or the connections and perishing of the flexible lines. Don't paint over rusty lines – that doesn't fool anyone and it could be dangerous. Replace them.

FRONT WHEEL BEARINGS

Worn front wheel bearings will reveal themselves by a whine or knocking whilst you are driving the car. It should be also possible to feel significant free play when the wheel is rocked side-to-side.

Speedometer cable location in the front-left wheel hub.

The front wheel bearing condition and play can be checked after the centre cap is removed (use a large screwdriver to prise the cap out, working around the circumference). On the left-hand wheel it will be necessary to clean off the sealing compound and remove the small circlip that retains the speedometer cable before removing the cap. After the cap is removed a clamping nut and thrust washer will be seen.

If the bearings are removed, check they are clean and fully wetted with about 30 gm or 2.2 oz of high-pressure grease, so that the stub axle cavity is largely filled. If the bearings are dry or contaminated with debris, renew them and completely clean the other components with clean fuel before repacking with grease. It is important the rear seal is also lubricated with grease, which should not be allowed to get on the brake pads or disc. Check the bearing journals for grooving. Grooves can cause grease leakage, which can then find its way onto the disc. If leakage has occurred and grooves are found, the stub axle or the disc may have to be replaced. To seat the bearings correctly on refitting, tighten the clamp nut, whilst turning the wheel, until resistance to rotation is felt continuously. Back the nut off half a turn and retighten until the thrust washer can just be moved sideways by lightly pressing with the blade of a screwdriver. Do not twist or lever the screwdriver to do this. There should be no detectable sideways play in the bearing, but the wheel should turn freely. When satisfied, tighten the socket-headed screw on the clamp nut to a torque of 13–16 Nm (9–11 lb ft). When refitting the left-hand bearing cap, set the speedo drive before tapping the cap back on with a soft hammer. Replace the circlip and cover with a silicone sealer.

On the 944, the socket-headed screw on the clamp nut has a fillister (12-point) head. A special tool is required to fit this type of screw, available from good suppliers or firms such as Snap-On Tools. The thread size is M7.

FRONT SHOCK ABSORBERS

Those cars fitted with Koni shock absorbers can be adjusted for damping rate. When replacement is necessary only the upper cartridge needs to be changed, not the whole unit. The factory colour code their dampers. The 924 models with a basic (soft) setting have a red paint coding; yellow paint is one turn harder (Turbo, CGT and 944 at launch); yellow with a blue spot is half a turn from basic (post-1982 944).

Only remove the complete strut unit if you have the equipment to check camber and toe-in, as loosening the two bolts which attach the strut to the kingpin also affects front wheel geometry.

The shock absorber should move smoothly up and down throughout its whole travel without sticking. If your car has had a rumbling or excessive pitching or rolling motion whilst driving, then it suggests the dampers should be replaced. Bounce each corner of the car – it should stop moving after one cycle (push down, rebound, settle). Any more movement and the damper should be replaced. Leakage from the strut also usually suggests replacement is necessary.

LOWER CONTROL ARM BALLJOINT

The control arm joints are riveted to the original pressed steel control arms and have VW Golf (Rabbit) heritage. To replace them, the rivets must be drilled out and the new joint

Original equipment control arms had their balljoints riveted to the metalwork.

Right: *On the same car, the other control arm joint has been replaced at some time.*

Strange steering effects can also come from (easily) bent lower control arms. This one shows evidence of straightening.

fitted with three HT M7 x 20 bolts, inserted downwards. The nut and bolt assemblies may be supplied with the replacement joint. Removing the rivets requires some careful drilling. A flat face of the hexagon bolt-head should face the joint, to prevent the head from rubbing the rubber boot of the joint. Changing the joint should not affect suspension geometry.

STEERING

Inspect the steering for excessive play in the balljoints and rack. Replace the balljoints if necessary, in the normal way. A balljoint 'cracker' will be required to release the taper-fitted joint. Tightening torque for the castle nut is 25 Nm (18.4 lb ft) and secure this nut after fitting with a new split pin. Inspect the steering rack boots for splits and seek advice if the boots look damaged.

944 steering has come in for a little criticism in that some cars have a noticeable steering shake. In most cases, this is due simply to out-of-round tyres, badly balanced tyres or dented/damaged rims. The less flexible the tyre wall is, the less likely the wheel will shake, so the later low pro-

file tyres on 16 inch rims are probably the best. There will be a reduction in ride comfort, though. The shake at the steering wheel can also be reduced by the flexible steering rod ends fitted on 1983-on 944 models.

The factory specifies zero toe-in, when the front wheels are loaded to 15 kg (34 lb) to simulate running conditions. Many workshops may not have the equipment to do this and it can be compensated for by adopting an unloaded figure of 3 mm ($\frac{1}{8}$ in).

Power steering is fitted to certain 944 models and works on the hydraulic assistance method. Its maintenance will not be discussed here, but if the steering makes a grunting noise when the wheel is turned it suggests the hydraulic fluid level is low. Low fluid lets air into the system, which can cause foaming. Before simply topping up, check around the components for leaks or damage. Consult a specialist for further help.

REAR AXLE

The rear suspension is very similar to the 911, in that each wheel is controlled by a trailing arm suspended by a torsion bar, and a shock absorber. The torsion bars are transverse and an anti-roll bar has been available as an option since the launch of the 924. The rear wheel camber is effectively not adjustable, although small changes are made when the ride height is adjusted. Toe can be altered by moving the trailing arms in their slots, where they mount to the torsion plates. This should only be done using the correct alignment equipment.

The rear axle height can be adjusted a small amount (without having to remove the torsion bars) by loosening the bolts on the two piece spring plates (1978-on). On the 944 the back end can be lowered by up to 25 mm (1 in) on US models. The height is adjusted by turning the rearmost eccentric bolt on the springplate, after loosening the single nut/bolt ahead of it. The camber will need checking after doing this.

To lower the car further means taking out the torsion bars and this is fully described in the Haynes Owners Workshop Manual on the 924.

Above: *Rear torsion bar tube of the 944. Note also the anti-roll bar and trailing arm mountings.*

Left: *The split rear spring plate on a 944. The rear anti-roll bar picks up on the 'camber' eccentric screw.*

The Carrera GT ride height was 15 mm lower than the 924 Turbo and used fabricated trailing arms that were strengthened around the wheel bearing and shock absorber mounting.

The rear brake assembly on a 944. Note the split pin locking the castellated nut that retains the wheel bearings.

REAR TORSION BAR/ANTI-ROLL BAR DATA

Type	Model Year	Torsion bar	Anti-roll bar	Option
924	launch to 1977	22mm	–	18mm
924	1978-on	22mm	–	–
924 option	1978-on	23.5mm	–	14mm

(23.5mm std on US/Canada/Japan models from 1981MY)

924 Turbo	launch-on	23.5mm	14mm	–

(Rear anti-roll bar only an option on US models)

924 CGT	launch-on	23.5mm	16mm	–
944	launch-on	23.5mm	14mm	–
944S	launch-on	23.5mm	18mm	–

(Optional torsion bar size of 24.5mm available)

944 Turbo S	launch-on	25.5mm	20mm	–

(Turbo Cup rear stabiliser is 21mm)

The adjuster for the parking brake is under the flexible boot, to the rear of the lever.

SHOCK ABSORBERS

See comments on front suspension for Koni colour codes

REAR DRIVE SHAFTS

Taking the drive shaft constant velocity joints apart is a specialist job, but if the rubber boots are split or damaged, the joints should be dismantled and fully cleaned. The joint should be replaced if there is too much radial play, which may have been detected by rear axle noises, when the car was being driven. Each joint should be packed with about 45 gm (1.6 oz) of molybdenum disulphide grease from both sides, a total of about 90 gm, (3.2 oz) per joint.

Tightening torque for the axle shaft flange bolts is 42 Nm (31 lb ft).

REAR BRAKES

Note the safety guidelines given previously in this chapter. If there are doubts about the brakes, consult a specialist. Drum brakes of 230 mm (9.1 in) diameter are fitted to the rear axle of all 924 and pre-1981 US 924 Turbo models. The brake linings can be inspected through the two holes in the backplate, near its rim. A new rear lining should be 3.8 mm–4.0 mm (0.15–0.16 in) thick and they should be replaced when the thickness is 2.5 mm (0.10 in).

The brake shoe position can be adjusted by turning a pinion, located in between the two shoes and accessed through a hole in the brake drum. Using a narrow-blade screwdriver, the pinion should be turned until the shoes prevent the drum from turning (parking brake off), and then backing the pinion off a little until the wheel turns freely.

Check the drum and brake lines for signs of fluid leakage. Leakage can come from rusty brake lines or perished or broken wheel cylinder seals. In all cases, replace the parts, being careful not to get any oil-based compound on the drum or linings.

The 924 Turbo, 944 and later 924S are fitted with 289 mm (11.26 in) ventilated disc brakes at the rear, using a single-pot floating caliper. See the discussion on the front disc brakes for inspection and maintenance guidelines.

The parking brake has separate cable-operated brake shoes acting on the disc hubs. It should be fully-on after four clicks of the lever. To adjust the parking brake, raise the rear of the car and plate it on axle stands. Remove the rear wheels and turn these to make sure the disc pads are not binding on the discs and that the discs turn freely with the parking brake off. Pull back the rubber boot on the brake lever, to reveal the adjuster. Loosen the nut so that there is no tension in the cable. The rear drum is then adjusted by positioning the approximately 10 mm (0.40 in) diameter hole in the disc hub at the highest point of its rotation, so that when a screwdriver is inserted through the hole, it can engage the small pinion adjuster on the end of the brake cylinder, inside the drum. Turn the adjuster until the disc cannot be moved and then back it off until it just turns freely. Refit the wheels. Back inside the car, pull up the brake lever two clicks and adjust the nut, so that the wheels can just be turned, but with effort. With four clicks the brake should then be fully effective. With the parking brake off there should be no brake resistance to rotation.

WHEELS

There are many different types of wheel that can be fitted to both the 924 and 944, both in steel and alloy. Ensure that any new wheel will physically fit under the wheel arch (with the tyre fitted). It should not foul the suspension or body or restrict the steering. This means the wheel offset should be the same as the standard wheel, if the rim size is the same. If you are fitting a wider wheel, the offset will need to be reduced by the increase in rim size. The offset is defined as the distance between the wheel centre face, where it fits to the hub, and the outer edge of the wheel rim. Be sure also that you are using the correct wheel nuts for the wheel (they are different for steel and alloy). For steel wheels on the four- and five-stud 924 hubs, the tightening torque is 110 Nm (81 lb ft). For alloy wheels on all models the torque is 130 Nm (96 lb ft). It is good practice to use a copper paste on the studs, to prevent later wheel nut seizing.

Only adhesive-type balance weights should be used on alloy wheels, not the clip types. They should be fitted only on the wheel's flat surfaces that are parallel to the axle line. This ensures the weight is pressed against the wheel at high speed, rather than having a tendency to be thrown off.

Finally, don't forget tyre pressures – they can noticeably affect the handling and rate of tyre wear.

Early 924 alloy wheel. The clip-type balance weight should not be used on alloy wheels.

A spoked alloy wheel fitted to a 924 Turbo as standard.

Refinished forged alloy wheel of traditional Porsche five-spoke design, fitted here to a Carrera GT.

A cast 'cookie-cutter' wheel on a 944.

Far left: *There was a mixed recep-
tion to the 'telephone dial' alloy
wheels.*

Left: *A machined finish seven-
spoke wheel, first seen on the 944
Turbo S.*

Later-style locking wheel nut.

CHAPTER 9

COMPETITION

The purpose of this chapter is not to present a glittering record of factory racing success, but to show that the front-engined Porsches can be the basis for enjoyable and competitive club racers. The basic cars are a very sound starting point for a competition vehicle because of the good weight distribution and body stiffness. The 924 especially can be prepared on a relatively low budget, yet will give a lot of driving fun. It has been shown to be fully class competitive in racing at club level in both the Porsche Club GB Challenge or in the more senior production Porsche championship. Although the precise regulations will differ, the same philosophies to Porsche 924 and 944 racing will apply internationally. Wherever you are your local Porsche club will be only too happy to point you in the direction of like-racing-minded owners.

From 1990 the PCGB Challenge offered the weekend or new racer the opportunity to race road-going Porsches in strictly regulated competition, where sponsorship is banned and no overall championship exists.

To quote the regulations the Challenge is 'intended to encourage Porsche owners to use their road cars for the purpose for which they have been developed and built, in a safe and controlled manner and to learn the basic skills of driving their Porsche in a friendly but competitive atmosphere'.

The discussion here will cover all aspects of 924 preparation necessary to produce a competitive car for the senior championship, but the same basic level of safety preparation and fine tuning can be applied to Challenge cars or, for that matter, any production racing series worldwide (with perhaps minor differences). The important aspect to remember about the Challenge is that most cars will

be used during the week and the level of competition is (purposely) not so intense. For the more ambitious the last section of this chapter covers 924 preparation for the UK racing series for modified Porsches.

PCGB SERIES REGULATIONS
All regulations change from year to year, but it will be useful firstly to understand the framework of the rules to see what is involved in preparing a production racing Porsche. I have presented below a summary of the regulations from the 1990 B.F. Goodrich/Porsche Club Great Britain Championship. I would say that for the Challenge, much of the detailed engine and chassis work can be ignored, but you will need to

Andy Monaghan's 924 finished fifth in Class D of the 1988 PCGB series.

take account of the safety rules. If you are serious about racing, contact the PCGB Motor Sport Division (address listed in the Appendices) to get the current regulations.

All cars must be roadgoing and fully legal to drive on the public highway.

WHEELS: Can be of any make, with any car allowed to fit 7J wheels or if 7J is the standard size, then 8J is allowed. Diameter must be standard.

TYRES: The only tyres permitted in the senior championship is the Goodrich Comp TAR1. This control tyre was introduced (successfully) in 1989 to keep tyre development costs manageable. Tyres must be treaded and road legal. Racing tyres are not permitted. Within the Challenge a selection of road tyres is permitted, complying with the RAC list of accepted types for production sports car racing.

BODYWORK: Must be standard for registered model, save that glass-fibre front wings and bonnets to standard profile are permitted. Only spoilers standard to the registered model may be fitted. 924 models may fit 924 Turbo pattern (but not 944) front and rear spoilers.

SUSPENSION: Unmodified standard suspension units, joints and bushes must be retained. Adjustment within scope of standard design is permitted. Shock absorber use is free, but the regulations state they must fit the original mounting points and no additional suspension facility (like coil spring assistance or adjustable spherical rod ends fitted to suspension arms) is permitted. Springs are free, but use of non-ferrous materials is prohibited. Any Porsche production anti-roll bars which fit the car without modification may be used. Adjustable links are not permitted.

BRAKES: Fluid and linings are free. Backing plates can be removed. Cooling hoses are permitted within body panels. Flexible hydraulic hoses are free.

INTERIOR: Subject to compliance with minimum overall weight limit. Replacement of driver's seat with a properly fixed racing seat is permitted. A properly trimmed passenger seat must be fitted (may be non-standard). Floor well carpets and hinged rear seats may be removed,

The driver's seat and steering wheel can be replaced. This is Steve Kevlin's 944S.

but all other trim including rear seat squabs and trimming on vertical surfaces must be in place. In 924 models the trunk area carpet may be replaced with lightweight trim. Substitute steering wheels are permitted. A 2.5kg minimum fire extinguisher must be fitted so that it can be reached by the strapped-in driver. Rear and diagonally braced roll-over bar and full seat harness are mandatory.

ENGINE: To standard UK specification for the registered model. Drive belts of engine driven pumps may be disconnected. No other modification is permitted and a variation of plus or minus 5 per cent of the published standard figure is applied to any output measurement. Turbo boost must not exceed standard UK specification for the registered model. Variable boost not permitted. Turbo over-boost light to be fitted (supplied by organisers). Air filters can be removed.

EXHAUST: Standard layout exhaust, including effective silencer boxes with standard outlets, must be used.

TRANSAXLE: All ratios must be as specified for the registered model.

FUEL: Only pump fuel is permitted.

WEIGHT: All vehicles must comply with the minimum weight limits

specified for the model. Weight is ready-to-race without petrol. Weight distribution to be as specified for model, plus or minus 1 per cent. In an effort to make a wider group of models competitive, the regulations have evolved each season so that there are exceptions to the permitted minimum weights or class eligibility. These changes have affected considerably the competitiveness of certain of the front-engined models.

924 PREPARATION

I am very grateful to Chris Turner, Steve Kevlin and Paul Smith for providing so much information on race preparation for the 924. The basic 924 falls into the 'D' class for Porsche cars not exceeding 140 bhp. The maximum permitted output for 924 is 125 bhp and minimum weight is 1000 kg (2205 lb). The maximum quoted torque (not a regulation) is 121 lb ft. The major competition in this class has been the 2.4 911T, which is allowed an output of 130 bhp at a weight of 1025 kg (2260 lb). Its quoted torque is 145 lb ft. In terms of power-to-weight ratio the two cars are virtually identi-

An external circuit breaker is not mandatory, but desirable.

Right: *Most competitors use cockpit decals to show the marshals how to turn things off quickly.*

An inertia reel passenger seat belt mounted off the 'C' pillar.

cal, although the 911T has better maximum torque. With correctly sorted suspension, the 924 may overcome this disadvantage with better cornering performance.

A good starting point is an early 924 with wind-up windows, but before you start searching for one of these now-rare models, read also the later section on gearboxes, because a five-speeder is essential.

A showroom 924 model in 1976 was 1080 kg (2370 lb); this had risen to 1185 kg (2607 lb) by 1980. The weight must be taken down to the 1000 kg (2205 lb) permitted by the regs to make full use of the permitted maximum 125 bhp. The minimum weight allowable is a concession in the regulations to allow the 924 to be more competitive. To

take 80 kg (176 lb) from an early 924 is a lot easier than removing 185 kg (408 lb) from a later model. The greater part of the weight increase is in sound-proofing, electrical equipment and additional trim. After all the visible sound-proofing is removed, including that under the carpets, bonnet and rear compartment, look at the interior trim and assess what can legally be removed. Electric windows can be replaced with wind-up versions, if the originally fitted type of mechanism is used. Lightweight racing seats will probably be necessary and aim to fit an alloy roll-over bar or cage. If the car has inertia-reel seat belts, these will have to be removed to fit a roll-over bar. A four-point (not a three-point) harness should be fitted to the driver's side. The child seat fittings in the back are suitable for the two rear straps and the front ones locate on the inertia unit mountings or directly to the floor. If the lap straps are fitted to the floor follow the manufacturer's instructions correctly to ensure a safe fitting. In the UK the car must pass

a roadworthiness check and this will mean a passenger seat belt must be fitted. Paul Smith used an old MGB inertia unit, fitted to the rear seat back mounting in the 'C' pillar.

With the 924 'lightweight rear trim' is permitted to extend to the rear seat area also. The aim should be that no bare metal is visible inside the car. Check with the organisers, though! Cars without sunroof are stiffer than those with, but a glass-fibre panel will reduce weight. Head-

An alloy roll-over bar and light-weight racing seat have been fitted in this 924.

Any unnecessary engine sheet metal can be removed. Note also the braided fuel injection lines.

linings must be retained but the sound-deadening material on the roof can be removed to lessen weight. If all this weight reduction still does not bring the car down to the weight limit, consider fitting glass-fibre wings and bonnet.

A limited amount of weight reduction can also be performed in the engine compartment with the removal of unnecessary sheet metal and air conditioning, if fitted.

BRAKES: Steel braid lines should be used for the flexible lines. Fit a new master cylinder, brake callipers and rear slave cylinders, if possible. The slave cylinders especially have a tendency to seize with age.

The rear brakes can also be cooled by fitting ducting, as long as the pipework stays inside the bodyshell.

To keep the front brakes cool, additional ducting can be routed from the radiator opening.

The beginner will probably not need to fit race pads/linings to start with, but as driving technique improves, the braking will become much more aggressive, leading to a high wear rate. In the UK the standard racing brake pad is the Ferodo DS11 and these should be fitted at least to the front brakes. Be aware that they will cause a sharp increase in the wear of the brake discs, which will probably need replacing every two or three seasons. Chris Turner has found ATE competition pads are easier on the discs than DS11 pads.

Standard brake fluid is unsuitable for any level of racing. Racing fluid should be changed at the start of every season.

One set of pads should last a season (because the brakes are not used much in a racing 924!). Paul Smith noted that fitting racing pads all-round to his 924 Turbo made the back end a little 'nervous' under heavy braking and he found that refitting the standard street pads at the back gave more predictable behaviour. Racing brake fluid only should be used. Standard fluid will boil within a few laps of hard use and silicone fluids give an unsatisfactory (spongy) pedal.

SUSPENSION: Assuming a good engine and driver, the influence of the suspension on the competitiveness of the car is total. To achieve the best handling, whilst staying inside the regulations, takes a lot of study and testing. It also needs an understanding of how you want the car to handle to bring out the best in your driving style.

Firstly, the free play in the suspension must be reduced to a minimum by fitting new front and rear wheel bearings and new flexible bushes throughout the suspension.

Front and rear anti-roll bars were an option on the 924 from the start, so look for these to be fitted on the basic car when you are buying. The 924 Turbo set up is probably a good starting point for anti-roll bar sizes (23mm f/14mm r). Chris Turner uses 20mm f/15mm rear to compensate for the basic car's pronounced understeering characteristic. The Carrera GT used a 16mm rear stabiliser. The roll stiffness should be increased to compensate for the standard car's soft springs, that give it an acceptable smooth ride for street use and also result in a significant amount of body roll. The anti-roll bars let the driver set the car up to understeer (with the stiffer front bar) or oversteer (a stiffer rear bar). The basic 924 understeers quite badly, so stiffening the rear anti-roll bar tends to counteract this.

The early cars were fitted with Boge or Koni front shock absorbers and Koni rears. Konis were fitted all round from 1980. The yellow Koni Sport dampers are an acceptable all-round fitting. Bilsteins can be fitted, but they are a more expensive option.

To keep the outside tyre flat on the road, given a relatively high degree of body roll in corners, the wheel will need negative camber. If this extra negative is not present, the outside tyre will roll outwards and the car will understeer on the reduced contact patch. It may result in faster (and unequal) wear of the tyre, but the

Running negative camber will mean greater wear on the inner shoulder of the tyre.

front suspension should be adjusted statically to between 3 and 3.5 degrees negative. Lowering the suspension is reasonably straightforward, but should be done using the right equipment. At the rear of pre-1978 cars, the ride height is adjusted as on the 911, by the eccentric bolts on the spring plates. On later cars the suspension should be removed to adjust rear ride height. At the front the coil springs should be cut to reduce ride height. The amount will be a matter of trial and error, but don't cut off too much! The car will settle after a run, so drive it after each new cut, to check the new height.

The suspension chapter has given all the data on torsion bar and coil spring sizes that are available to the production racer. The accepted fit is to have Carrera GT front springs with the standard 22 mm or 23.5 mm rear torsion bars.

WHEELS AND TYRES: You can go up to 7J rims with 205/55 maximum tyres. With Comp T/A-type tyres, one set should last a season. For a front runner, it will be necessary to run buffed tyres, where the tread is cut down to a mere 2-3 mm (0.1 in) depth (what a waste of a new tyre!).

The Goodrich TAR tyres are supplied with only 4 mm tread depth.

Right: *Good practice when using alloy wheels in racing is to keep them clear of brake dust (it can cause pitting and eventual stress failure), to use screw-in valves (less chance of leakage) and to use stick-on balance weights (again does not scratch wheel).*

Below: *Australian Paul Smith's Turbo has been extensively modified. The car shows off its 7J 928 wheels and lowered suspension.*

This is to prevent what is called 'block squirm' where the tread blocks move around due to the tremendous heat generated during hard cornering. Goodrich also claim this block movement can inhibit rainwater drainage during cornering and eventually cause aquaplaning. The Comp TAR tyre is not recommended for the Challenge as it will wear too quickly. The suggested alternative is the Comp TA, although the tyre manufacturer is not restricted. For the 924, the 7x15 rims should be used, with 205/50 VR15 tyres. Paul Smith uses standard 928 wheels and compensates for the change in offset with a small spacer. The spacer keeps the tyre from rubbing the suspension spring. 205 tyres can be fitted to the standard 6 inch rim, but the tread will not sit as flat on the road as with a 7 inch wheel.

The lower profile benefits the car's gearing on the shorter circuits. Inflation pressure is an easily adjusted variable that can have a lot of effect. Aim to run the lowest pressures possible, without the tyre rolling off the rim. It is important the tyre does not overheat, the B.F. Goodrich recommendation suggests 140-180°F (77-88°C) is best, with a maximum of 220°F (104°C). It seems trivial, but it's worth spending some time

Above: *The 928 7J next to a standard Turbo 6J. The tread presents a larger 'footprint' when fitted to the larger rim.*

Left: *To prevent the 7J wheel and tyre from fouling the front coil spring, a spacer is used. Note also the heavy disc marking from using competition brake pads.*

whilst testing to get the best tyre pressures sorted out.

ENGINE: A 924 engine will go off-tune more quickly than a 911 unit, because there is less tolerance to play with within the regulations. The engine should be tuned for a balance of performance and fuel economy. A rebuild is an essential starting point. Aim to replace the valve springs with new (standard) components. If the racing is serious, this may be worth doing mid-season also as the springs can age quite quickly especially if the four-speed gearbox is used (the

The Turbo oil cooler can be fitted to the standard 924, if oil temperature is a problem.

engine gets revved more). Valve guides should be as new, but not tight (the top tolerance is best). It is not permitted to polish the head but careful gasket matching, etc, should be done. The cylinder head can be skimmed to the lowest deck height permitted within drawing tolerances, but this is a special machining job, so consult a specialist first who has done it before.

Inside the engine, the requirement is minimum friction. This means honing the bores with 1000 grade dry paper, but not so much that blow-by of the piston rings will become a problem. The crankshaft should be crack-tested and preferably be of the standard size. It should be polished down to bottom specification to ensure free running bearings on both the mains and big ends.

Hone the bores, but not so much that piston ring blow-by becomes a problem.

It is also worth balancing the crank again as the factory balance can sometimes be less than perfect. If there is any doubt about the history of the crankshaft replace it.

All the critical engine bolts should be new, especially those securing the bearings, rods and cylinder head (they get stretched on one tightening).

The camshaft timing should be set up exactly at the optimum. A detail modification for the really serious racer is to use a vernier gauge to position the camshaft accurately to its drive pulley. Specially made-up keys are used to ensure the camshaft timing is exactly right. No two engines will be the same, due to variations in production tolerances.

The camshaft should be perfect condition, with no evidence of wear.

The fuel pressure can be increased by adjusting the control pressure (see Chapter 6) but if the car is driven home after the race, it would be wise to weaken the mixture back again to avoid excessive fuel consumption and bore washing.

The ignition system should be set up to the book, and then the fuel and ignition set using a rolling road. If oil temperature is a problem, then fit the 924 Turbo oil cooler to the

right of the coolant radiator (in the same place as the Turbo).

GEARBOX: It is essential to have a five-speed gearbox if you are serious about winning and for most the post-1980 type 016/8 or 9 unit is best. Ideally this will have the optional limited slip differential fitted. Wheelspin is not something the 924 driver has to worry about often, but the diff can be useful if the car lifts an inside wheel or there is slip coming out of wet bends. Although not relevant to the British series, a diff would be useful also if slicks were used. A very experienced driver might go for the earlier gearbox (type 016Z or Y) which has the gear cluster ahead of the axle line. The polar moment of inertia is reduced and as a result, the dynamic response of the car may be better.

Certain light gear oils will reduce transmission losses, but be ready for increased wear.

CLUTCH: This remains standard, but new parts should be used throughout. Removing the bottom plate from the bellhousing will improve air circulation around the clutch, even if you don't like the smell!

The main point with engine (and its systems) tuning is that even if the output comes out too high, this can be adjusted by timing or fuel metering to bring it back under the +5 per cent.

The skill of driving a 924 competitively is based on keeping one's right foot firmly on the floor for as much of the lap as possible. The driving style is similar to Formula Ford, where comparatively low engine output is partially balanced by a chassis that handles well. Because the car is slow out of bends, the art is to maintain as much momentum as possible through them. Such a driving style can be quite alarming to follow, especially in a production spec 911, which generally must slow up more for a given bend. The 924 is much more predictable than the 911 through bends and is a good car if you are new to racing. The right 924 in the right hands is competitive with equivalent class 911 types and is an inexpensive way of going racing.

924 TURBO

The 177 bhp 924 Turbo is in the next class up in the British production series (Class C: 141 bhp to 180 bhp).

This standard VDO boost gauge can replace the clock in the 924 Turbo.

Everything that has been said for the standard 924 is appropriate for the Turbo. The unfortunate aspect is that this car's minimum weight is 1100 kg (2426 lb), 100 kg (220 lb) more than the unblown car. The 924 Turbo has a struggle in Class B against the 2.4-litre 911E, which has 165 bhp and has a minimum weight of 995 kg (2194 lb). There may be a case for some regulation 'evolution'

The Turbo will benefit from this additional oil supply to the cylinder head, that improves valve cooling and lubrication.

to permit further weight reduction. After all, the showroom weight for 2.4 911E was 1075 kg (2370 lb). The only 911 ever to weigh as little as 995 kg was the 1968 911S.

Paul Smith and Colin Mowle have shown that the 924 Turbo can be a lot of fun to race, since it offers a fair degree of performance for the money, with good reliability.

944

From 1990 the 2.5-litre 944 has been eligible for Class D, the same class as the 924. With 163 bhp and a permitted minimum weight of 1190 kg (2624 lb), it has a greater power to weight ratio and maximum torque than the previous chief contender in the class, the 2.4 911T. With early 944s now freely available on the second-hand market, this could be a serious competitor.

944S

The 190 bhp 2.5-litre 944S is accepted in Class C at a weight of 1145 kg (2525 lb). With access to the Porsche Cars GB 'parts bin', Steve Kevlin first raced a specially prepared

944S in 1988.

The 2.5-litre 944S he drove had the Club Sport package and a mildly blueprinted engine. As with the 924, skill and experience is vital for setting up the suspension. To get the permitted 8J rear rims under the rear arches, he used wheels with less offset than standard, so reducing the rear track. This allowed some flexibility in selecting tyre sizes. The car started with the standard 7Jx15 wheels, with 205 front and 225 rear tyres, but this gave lower gearing. 16 inch wheels allowed 245 rears to be tried, which kept heat levels under control at some circuits. Generally, the lower gearing from running low profile tyres on the 15 inch rims made these undesirable at the rear and the best overall configuration has been 205/15s at the front and 225/16s at the rear.

For 1989, the 944S was upgraded to S2 specification, with a full 3-litre engine. It was eligible in Class B of the now-Goodrich sponsored championship. Eight class wins and four seconds was enough to win him what had become a very serious and professional series. Preparing a 944S2 to win would not be a small budget operation.

With only 400 built, the 924 Carrera GT has not been competitively raced in the series discussed here. It would be eligible in the same class as the 944S2 and on paper seems more competitive. With values rising rapidly owners of original models are not too keen on risking them! Replicas are permitted but none have raced, yet.

Steve Kevlin's 1988 2.5-litre 944S was upgraded to full S2 spec. With 3-litre power he won the Goodrich PCGB Production Porsche Championship in 1989.

Below: *The 944S engine looks virtually standard from the exterior.*

Under the rear of Tiff Needell's 944 Turbo 'S'. Note the cast trailing arms, adjustable dampers and buffed tyres.

944 TURBO SPORT

This model was shown to be a winner in 1988 in the hands of Tiff Needell, in the top British production class (cars over 208 bhp). The competitiveness of the Porsche Cars GB-entered car was shown by the fact that it won at both the fast tracks (Silverstone and Zandvoort) and at the relatively twisty ones (Oulton Park and Brands Hatch). This suggests the car is good in the right hands to become an overall winner with a little more development. Steve Kevlin says the car that Needell used was built from 'the best of the parts bin' and had a blueprinted engine. Otherwise its spec is Turbo Cup. Its competition has been the Carrera RS with 210 bhp and a weight of 995 kg (2194 lb) and the 3.3-litre 930 Turbo with 330 bhp and 1400 kg (3087 lb). Compare this with the 250 bhp and 1240 kg (2734 lb) of the 944T and it's time to get the calculator out! The car certainly trails the 930 in power-to-weight ratio and I'm sure Needell's extensive driving experience made up for the shortfall in 1988. A less experienced driver may not get the same degree of success. It is also relevant that the early 1970s 911 models have a good ten or more years' head start on the 944 Turbo in their development for racing. The 944 Turbo would look a lot more competitive if its engine acquired sixteen valves or another 500cc! Again, the 944 Turbo is a big-budget racer.

MODIFIED RACING

Only the preparation of the production four-cylinder models has been considered so far, because it is the easiest way to go Porsche racing at a reasonable budget. The UK has seen an explosion of interest in Porsche racing in the mid-eighties and there are now both production and modified series to choose from.

Many enthusiasts are turning to the modified series, to produce cars which are more strongly tuned and are more exciting to drive.

This is the path that Paul Smith's 924 Turbo has followed. He was fortunate enough to acquire enough parts to begin converting his 924 Turbo to Carrera GTS specification, with the intention of racing the reborn car in the Porsche Club GB's Modified championship. The accompanying photographs give an idea of the degree of the conversion. It can be just as enjoyable building up a car like this for competition as racing it. This 'GTS' was no exception.

The components came from a proposed one-off that Porsche specialists Autofarm prepared in the UK in the early eighties. The suspension features solid bushing throughout, with acetal being the preferred bushing material. The suspension attachments were solid mounted also, through spherical joints and the anti-roll bars

were adjustable front and rear. The intention was to use original GTR brake disc units, with alloy hubs and four-pot calipers. The suspension was strengthened and GTS torsion bars were used front and rear. The body-work was lightened extensively using glass-fibre parts for the bonnet, doors and wings. A GTR-spec. Plexiglas rear tailgate comes from the States and a lightweight engine undertray improves underbody airflow.

The engine will be brought to GTS specification, using a Carrera GT intercooler and suitably increased turbocharger boost. A Neil Bainbridge Racing 'big-bore' throttle housing will be fitted. This is a conversion that improves the airflow to the cylinders.

The car will be an interesting change from the many hot 911 models seen in the modified series. There is no reason to assume it will not be competitive, if the original GTS power figure of 245 bhp can be duplicated.

Right: *Paul Smith's "GTS" project features solid bushed suspension. This is a lower control arm with adjustable anti-roll linkage.*

Below: *The complete rear suspension assembly, with solid bushed trailing arms (where they fit to the torsion bar tube).*

The rear anti-roll bar is completely adjustable, with spherical joints.

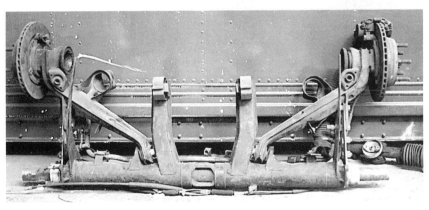

Right: *A cast rear suspension bearing flange, showing the solid bush in place of the standard flexible item.*

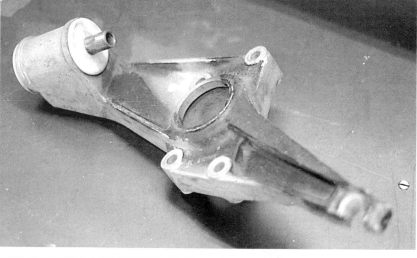

Above: *A GTR front stub-axle assembly. The grooves on the disc help clear brake dust and water from the face.*

Right: *The outer face of the stub-axle, showing the efforts made to reduce (unsprung) weight.*

Above: *A four-pot caliper from the GTR.*

Left: *A single-throat throttle assembly, which has been extensively modified.*

152

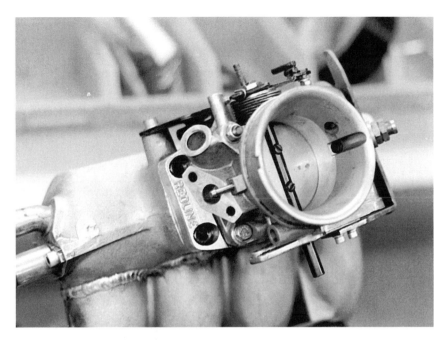

The air distributor has been gas-flowed internally and the unit rewelded. Note that this assembly is for the GTR, where the turbo is on the left side of the engine.

Below left: *Playing with the turbo boost can be expensive. This cylinder head shows evidence of piston ring breakage. Note also the heavy pitting in the combustion chamber (low grade fuel?) and the poor condition of the valve seats.*

Below: *In the corner of the workshop sits a lightweight aluminium engine undertray and a plexiglass rear tailgate.*

SPECIFICATIONS

These listings have been prepared from the original launch specifications published by the factory. The method used will be to give the original specification of the 2-litre 924 and then continue, model year by model year, showing only changes made from the previous year. Model years run from the August preceding the year designated to the following August (ie a 1982 model year car could have been sold in August 1981). Note that because of space limitations, external colour and interior trim changes have generally not been recorded here.

924 1976/7

Start of production: November 1975. USA launch: April 1976, but known as 1977 model. UK launch 10 March 1977 (RHD).

Chassis

Bodywork: two-door coupé, 2 + 2 with rear opening hatch. Longlife 6-year anti-corrosion guarantee on under-body. US models have safety bumpers and large side repeaters ahead of front wheels, amongst other regulatory details. Ground clearance 150 mm (5.9 in).
Frame: Unitary steel construction with bolt-on front wings.
Front suspension: Independent, lower control arms with MacPherson principle coil spring/double action shock absorbers.
Rear suspension: Independent, angled trailing arms with transverse torsion bars and double acting hydraulic shock absorbers. Anti-roll bars: optional front and rear.
Steering: Rack and pinion, ratio 19.15:1. 4.0 turns lock-to-lock. Turning circle 9.24 m (30.3 ft).
Brakes: twin-circuit hydraulic, split diagonally, with boost. Disc front (256.5 mm/10.1 in), drum rear (231x38 mm/9.1x1.5 in).
Wheels: Pierced steel 5.5Jx14, or optional pressure cast 6Jx14.

Tyres: Steel rims, 165 HR14; cast rims, 185/70 HR14.

Transmission Transaxle unit with front engine and rear mounted gearbox, bolted together as a rigid drive line unit by means of a torque tube. Torsionally elastic drive shaft (20 mm) in four bearings.
Clutch: Single dry-plate within engine bellhousing.
Gearbox: Type YR (088/6) fully synchronised 4-speed manual, sharing housing with the differential. Shift lever mounted on the drive tunnel. Double-joint drive shafts to rear wheels with length compensation. (Numbers after YR designation refer to production date (for example YR19027 was made on 19 Feb '77).

Gear	Teeth	Ratio
1	10/36	3.6000:1
2	16/34	2.1250:1
3	25/34	1.3600:1
4	30/29	0.9667:1
Final drive 9/31		3.4444:1

Engine

Bore x Stroke: 86.5 x 84.4 mm.
Capacity: 1984 cc (121.06 cu in). Compression: Europe, 9.3:1; US/Canada/Japan, 8.0:1.
Aluminium alloy crossflow cylinder head with Heron-type combustion chambers. Forged steel connecting rods (plain bearings) and cast aluminium pistons with 2 compression/ 1 oil scraper rings. Iron block with aluminium sump pan.
Crankshaft: Forged steel with 5 plain main bearings.
Valves: Overhead in-line, 2 per cylinder. Intake: 40 mm (US 38 mm), exhaust: 33 mm. Overhead camshaft and cup followers. Toothed belt drive.
Lubrication: Pressure lubrication by Sichel cogwheel pump. Main stream oil filter.
Fuel system: Electric fuel pump and Bosch K-Jetronic fuel-

injection. Octane requirement: 98 RON.
Electric system: 12 volt, 45 Ah battery with 1050 watt alternator. European models; conventional coil ignition; US models, transistorised ignition.

Output: European version:	125 bhp DIN/119 SAE at 5800 rpm.
	121.5 lb ft torque at 3500 rpm.
US/Canada/Japan:	100 bhp DIN/95.4 SAE at 5500 rpm. 109 lb ft at 4000 rpm.

Dimensions
Wheelbase: 2400 mm (94.5 in)
Front track: 1418 mm (55.8 in)
Rear track: 1372 mm (54.0 in)
Length: 4216.4 mm (166.0 in)
Width: 1686.6 mm (66.4 in)
Height: 1270 mm (50.0 in)

Capacities
Fuel tank: 13.8 Imp gal 18.7 US gal/66 l (includes 1.0 Imp gal/1.3 US gal/4.55 l reserve).
Engine oil: 7 Imp p/4.2 US qt/4 l.
Radiator: approx. 1.53 Imp gal/7.4 US qt/7 l.
Gearbox: 4.58 Imp pt/2.75 US qt/2.6 l, hypoid SAE 80.
Brake reservoir: 0.33 Imp pt/0.2 qts US/0.19 l.
Windscreen washer: 3.5 Imp pt/2.1 US qt/2 l.
Headlamp washer: 11.3 Imp pt/6.8 US qt/6.4 l.

Weights
Empty (DIN): 2380 lb (1080 kg)
Permitted total: 3085 lb (1400 kg)

Performance

European:	0–62 mph, (0–100 km/h), 10.5 secs. Standing start Km, 32.2 sec. Top speed, 125 mph (200 km/h).
US:	0–60 mph, 11.9 secs. Top speed 111 mph (68.93 km/h).

Prices/options
1976 West Germany: DM23240 ($8900), base model.
1976 USA: $9395 base model.
Optional equipment: Removable roof panel $330, air conditioning $548, front/rear sway bars $105, metallic paint $295, 3 speaker radio $105. Touring package 1 (triple speakers, leather steering wheel, 6 inch alloy wheels): $345. Touring Package 2 (headlamp washers, rear wiper, passenger door mirror): $240.
1977 UK: £6999 base model.
Optional equipment: Automatic three-speed transmission (see US 1977½ model for ratios), tinted glass, 6Jx14 alloy wheels, front/rear anti-roll bars, detachable roof panel, headlamp washers, rear wiper, leather steering wheel. Celebration model: Total batch of 2000, of which 100 RHD UK models 'fully equipped' and special colour scheme (white with red/white/blue flash in Martini race car style). Identified internally by centre console plaque, deep plpe red carpets and specially upholstered corduroy seats.
Price in UK – £7673. All 924 models receive roller blind cover in rear luggage area for 1977.

924 1977½ (USA only)
Engine output raised (compression ratio up from 8.0 to 8.5:1), increased intake valve size from 38 mm to 40 mm, changed camshaft/ignition timing. Output now 110 bhp SAE at 5750 rpm. Rear axle ratio changed from 3.44 to 3.89:1 (9/35). All cars now have catalytic converters. Auto transmission is optional in March 1977, coded RK in Europe (RL in USA in brackets below).

Range	Teeth	Ratio
1		2.552:1
2		1.448:1
D		1.000:1
R		2.462:1
Final drive	11/38 (11/41)	3.455:1 (3.727:1)

924 1978
Oval exhaust tailpipe, introduced, improved noise suppression. Longer life brake pads (claimed reduced dust transfer to front wheels). 6.4-litre water container now serves both windshield and headlamp washers. Pile carpet replaces loop weave of previous year. Herringbone upholstery and trimmed rear seats. Interior vinyl facings have grained texture. UK models have front/rear anti-roll bars, leather steering wheel and built-in rear fog lights as standard. 924 Lux introduced in UK grouping most popular options (alloy 6J wheels and wider tyres, tinted windows, rear wiper and headlamp washers).
Getrag pattern 5-speed gearbox with dog-leg first gear

optional. Code letters 016Z/VA (Europe, RoW), Code 016Y/VB (USA, shown in brackets below). All codes followed by 5 digit number, giving date of manufacturer. Oil volume is 2.5 litres hypoid SAE80.

Gear	Teeth	Ratio
1	14/39 (14/39)	2.786:1
2	18/31 (19/32)	1.722:1 (1.684:1)
3	23/28 (27/30)	1.217:1 (1.111:1)
4	29/27 (31/25)	0.931:1 (0.806:1)
5	34/24 (35/21)	0.706:1 (0.600:1)
R	46/21 (16/14)	2.503:1
Rear axle	7/33 (7/35)	4.714:1 (5.000:1)

Sports shock absorbers optional.
U.K. price: 924 £7350, 924 Lux £7800.

924 1979

6J alloy wheels with 185/70 HR14 tyres standard. Space-saver spare wheel (except UK). Cloth inserts for door panels, vanity mirror on passenger visor and stereo speakers (but no radio!) standard. In UK, 924 Lux gets electric windows and electrically operated and heated driver's door mirror as standard. Options include black enamel spokes with polished rims to wheels.
Prices: UK 924 £8199, 924 Lux £8649, auto £449 extra. USA: 924 $11995. Options (not exhaustive list): metallic paint $395, air conditioning $595, AM/FM stereo radio $150, sway bars $150, Touring Package 1 $520, Convenience Package 2 $1270 (incl AM/FM stereo/cassette and electric windows/mirror, etc.), sunroof $380, tinted glass $105, California emissions equipment $110.

924 1980

New 5-speed gearbox with 911 pattern standard (5th speed to right and forward of 'H'). Gearbox type 016/8 coded VQ for Europe, RoW. Type 016/9 code VR for USA/Japan. Transistor ignition now standard on Europe, RoW models. Larger 9 inch brake servo means lower pedal pressure. 911SC-type 3-spoke steering wheel. Black-look window surrounds. Auto light in luggage compartment. Flap over petrol cap, black side trim strips and Porsche lettering above rear bumper. In UK 924 Lux gets choice of tartan, chequer-board velours or plaid seat materials, more sound proofing, carpeting on sides of centre console. Exterior sills have plastic covers for protection and door sills have black decals with '924' motif. Options include two-tone paint and electric passenger door mirror. In US new 3-way catalyst and oxygen sensor fitted to basic model, plus supplementary fuel pump fitted in fuel tank. Limited edition 'Sebring '79' series of

1300: bright red with black, white and gold stripes.

Prices: UK 924 £9103, 924 Lux £9581, auto plus £478 both models.
USA 924 $15970 basic. Options: Handling package (incl 4-wheel disc brakes, large diam etc front and rear anti-roll bars, leather steering wheel, sports shock absorbers and alloy wheels with P7 tyres).

924 1981

Additional noise damping, standard front anti-roll bar, stiffer rear torsion bars. Braided injection lines and new fuel pump with check valve on outlet. Brake fluid level indicator added. Small side repeater lights ahead of doors and rear fog light on European models. Carpeting to centre console, 924 Turbo horn, new control symbols, new steering column lever and embossed Porsche lettering on door panels standard. Options include Blaupunkt QTS cassette/radio, cassette holder, Berber all-cloth seats or all leather seats. Full seven year anti-corrosion guarantee over whole body.
Prices: UK 924 £9103, 924 Lux £9582.
In Europe, limited edition 'Le Mans': white with gold/red/black stripes with 924 Turbo rear spoiler, sport shock absorbers, rear anti-roll bar, alloy (924 Turbo) wheels with 205/60 HR15 tyres. Lift-out sunroof, PDM and pinstripe interior standard. 100 imported to UK at price of £10600.
In US limited edition of 400 'Weissach' models in single metallic platinum colour. Same mechanical spec as European 'Le Mans' model, except has tweed interior and air conditioning. Price: $19500.
From 1981 Europe. RoW models fitted with 016/8 code MD gearbox and, when fitted with LSD, coded 4Q. For US, fitted with 016/9 code MF (shown in brackets below) and when fitted with LSD became code 5Q. For Japan models only fitted with 016/9 code ME.

Gear	Teeth	Ratio
1	10/36	3.600:1
2	16/34	2.125:1
3	24/35 (25/34)	1.458:1 (1.360:1)
4	28/31 (30/29)	1.107:1 (0.966:1)
5	35/30 (37/27)	0.857:1 (0.729:1)
R	12/42	3.500:1
Rear axle	9/35 (9/37)	3.889:1 (4.111:1)

924 production for USA, Canada and Japan ceases at end of 1981.

924 1982

Carpeting on restyled door pockets and Porsche badge on glove compartment latch. Roof reinforced so that roof load of 75 kg (165 lb) is permitted with the 'Porsche carrier system'. Capacity of the fresh air vents increased by redesigning the air control flap system. Limited slip differential and sport suspension pack (uprated shock absorbers and larger diameter anti-roll bars) offered as options. UK price: 924 £9103, 924 Lux £9582.

924 1983

Flexible rear spoiler around tailgate now standard. Two front mounted loudspeakers increased from 5 to 15 watts. 924 Turbo spoke-effect alloy wheels/60-series tyres and stoneguard spats now an option. Synchromesh on reverse gear and improved interior sound proofing. Provision for four speaker radio system. Prices: UK 924 £9494 (plus £499 for auto), 924 Lux £9993.

924 1984

Electric rear tailgate release standard, electric tilt facility for sunroof optional. Interior cloth trim has woven-in Porsche motif in choice of black, brown and grey beige for seat inlays. New rear seat backrest release. Optional Turbo style 6J wheels with 205/60 HR15 tyres get locking wheel nuts. Prices: UK 924 £11353 (plus £511 extra for auto), 924 Lux £11996.

924 1985

Launch 1 October 1984 (see text).
Electrically heated windshield washer nozzles standard. Graduated top tint for windshield optional. Prices: UK 924 £11568 (plus £469 extra for auto), 924 Lux £12123.

924S 1986

August 1985 first details of the 2.5-litre engined 924S released. Replaces 2-litre 924 in marketplace from early 1986.
Engine: Water-cooled, 4-cylinder in-line unit with overhead camshaft.
Bore x stroke x 78.9 mm. Displacement 2479 cc, compression ratio 9.7:1, output 150 bhp DIN at 5800 rpm. Torque 144 lb ft at 3000 rpm. 91/82 RON fuel (leaded or unleaded), digital engine electronics. 12 volt 50 Ah battery, 90A generator. Performance identical with or without catalytic converter.
Performance: 0–100 km/h (0–62.5 mph) in 8.5 seconds, top speed 214 km/h (133 mph).
External changes: Pressure cast 'telephone dial' wheels (6Jx15 with 195/65 VR15 tyres). Option is forged 6Jx16 wheels with 205/55 VR16 tyres. Ventilated disc brakes all round, plug light alloy semi-trailing arms from 944. Interior changes: driver's seat set higher with 363 mm steering wheel (was 380 mm). Taller drivers can remove spacers. Power steering now standard with auto model. Light grey and fine pinstripe flannel cloth replaces grey/beige and velour check interior trim. Otherwise interior/dash same as previous 924 (ie not 'oval' 944 dash). 924S launched in USA mid-1986. Standard are heated outside mirrors, power steering, air conditioning, four speakers, powered antenna, cassette holder (but no radio!) and wheel locks.

Prices: UK 924S £14985 (plus £1055 extra for auto/power steering).
USA 924S basic $19900 (Compare this with 924 'Weissach' model of 1981!).

924S 1987

In UK Panasonic CQ877 digital self-seek radio/cassette with four speakers and auto antenna standard. Passenger door mirror and battery operated light in key fob standard. Sport seats now available as option. Prices: UK 924S £17484 (with £1312 extra for 3-speed auto).

924S 1988

160 bhp/210 lb ft (DIN) 944 engine fitted to give top speed 137 mph (220 km/h) and 0–100 km/h (0–62 mph) in 8.2 secs. Engine runs on 95 RON petrol. Power steering standard on UK models (plus cassette holder, coin rack and rear stone spats). Split rear seat backrest with 'special' luggage cover which lifts with tailgate an option. Limited edition 'Le Mans' model available. In UK only 74 to be sold, with half in Alpine white and half in black. Comes with Sport suspension, which includes lower ride height, gas shock absorbers, harder springs and larger rear anti-roll bar (up from 14 mm to 20 mm). 7J wheels fitted (colour coded highlights match interior colours). White cars get grey/ochre flannel striped cloth Sports seats. Black cars have grey/turquoise. 'Le Mans' script on each side of car.
924 discontinued at August 1988.

924 Turbo 1979

Only differences from the 1979 924 will be listed.
European launch March 1979 (first details released November 1978). USA launch September 1979, UK launch, November 1979.
Porsche internal designation is model number 931.

Engine: Compression ratio 7.5:1. Cast pistons. Cylinder head redesigned (recess in combustion chamber roof, platinum tipped plugs on 'other' side). Inlet valve 40 mm, exhaust 36 mm. Breakerless transistor ignition. KKK turbocharger fitted downstream of exhaust manifold with bypass valve and wastegate (max. boost 0.65 bar). Sump pan oil cooler modified. Oil capacity now 5.5 litres (9.9 Imp pt or 5.83 US qt). Bosch K-Jetronic fuel meter and alternator relocated. Larger diameter fuel lines and second fuel pump (at exit from tank) fitted. Fuel 98RON. Output is 170 bhp DIN at 5500 rpm, max torque 180 lb ft at 3500 rpm. Transmission: Gearbox is type G31 5-speed, effectively the 924 016Z,Y modified for greater torque. Still with 'dog-leg' first gear. Fitted as G31/01 from launch for Europe, RoW. Until end 1980 MY fitted as G31/02 to USA/Japan models (in brackets below). Oil is changed to Hypoid SAE90.

Gear	Teeth	Ratio
1	12.38	3.167:1
2	18/32	1.778:1
3	23/28	1.217:1
4	29/27	0.931:1
5	34/24 (35/21)	0.706:1 (0.600:1)
R	12/16 – 22/48	2.909:1
Rear axle	8/33 (7/33)	4.125:1 (4.714:1)

Torque shaft increased by 5 mm to 25 mm diameter. Clutch increased by 10 mm to 225 mm diameter with hydraulic operation (was cable).
Suspension: Koni replaces Boge shock absorbers at front, 23 mm (was 22 mm) front anti-roll bar. At rear Bilstein shocks fitted with 14 mm (was 18 mm) anti-roll bar. Wheel hubs and bearings from 911SC.
Steering: Rack/pinion ratio now 20:1 (was 19.1:1).
Brakes: Europe, 4 wheel ventilated discs (282.5 mm/11.1 in front, 289 mm/11.4 in rear) with 928 calipers.
Wheels: Spoke-style cast alloy 6Jx15 with 5-stud fixing.
Exterior: Integrated rear tailgate spoiler, NACA duct in bonnet (hood) and additional vents in panel between headlamps and in front spoiler. Two-tone colour scheme available as option.
Interior: Steering wheel 5 mm smaller at 378 mm. Instruments have green figures. Leather gear lever gaiter. UK models have Panasonic CQ-8600, electric antenna, tinted windows, headlamp washers and rear wiper as standard. Weight: 2614 lb (1180 kg) (DIN) (924 was 2492 lb/1130 kg).
Performance: Top speed, (factory) 140 mph (225 km/h),

real figure could be 5-10 mph higher. 0–100 km/h (0–62 mph), 7.8 secs.
US market features: Smaller turbo with three-way converter. 143 bhp SAE at 5500 rpm, max torque 147 lb ft at 3000 rpm. Fuel is unleaded 91RON. Gearbox changes (in brackets above) give overall shorter gearing. Steering ratio 22.4:1. American spec bumpers fitted and retains disc front/drum rear brakes. Options include 'S' package with 4-wheel ventilated disc brakes, 5-stud wheel fixings, 928-style alloy wheels with Pirelli P7 tyres (against the standard CN36), stiffer shock absorbers, 23 mm (was 21 mm) front anti-roll bar and 14 mm rear anti-roll bar. Weight is 2835 lb (1287 kg). USA approx. top speed 129 mph (207 km/h) with 0–60 mph in 9.3 seconds.

Prices: UK £13629
USA $20875 50-State basic (excls rear wiper, radio, air conditioning, sunroof, etc). 'S' option $2045, E-32 option (air conditioning, removable roof panel, electric door mirrors) $1500, 2-tone paint $895, rear wiper $235. Radio/cassette still an option.

924 Turbo 1980
No change for European LHD models. USA and UK launch types became 1980 models (but include new 1980 new paint range).

924 Turbo 1981
European/UK output raised to 177 bhp at 5500 rpm, max torque 185 lb ft at 3500 rpm. Compression ratio 8.5:1. Equipped with Siemans-Hartig digital ignition system. Smaller turbo unit (now same for all markets). Significant improvement in fuel consumption. Better crankcase breathing, to improve after-shutdown oil circulation (and thus turbo life). Single large butterfly replaces previous two in throttle housing. Piston recess is revised. New flywheel/clutch and metal fittings to fuel injectors (were plastic). Side repeater flashers in front of doors fitted. White figures (were green) on instruments. Rear fog light for European models. Brake fluid indicator. Porsche lettering embossed on door panels. New control lever on steering column. Fuel tank increased to 84 l/22 US gal/18.5 Imp gal. Longlife guarantee extended to seven years for entire body unit.
US version becomes 154 bhp SAE at 5500 rpm with 155 lb ft at 3300 rpm. Compression ratio is 8.0:1. Final drive ratio now 3.89:1. Performance is 127 mph (204 km/h) and 0-60 in 9.2 secs *(Road & Track)*. Ventilated disc brakes

fitted all round. Gearbox now 016G, coded MB for USA and MX for Japan. Ratios are as 016/8 European except fifth speed, which is same as 016/9. Rear axle same as European version.

Prices: UK £13998
            USA $21500 basic (incl air cond, alloy wheels).

924 Turbo 1982
New upholstery, carpeted door pockets and Porsche crest on glove compartment latch. Reinforced roof. 16 inch 928-style wheels an option. Price: unchanged from 1981. 924 Turbo ceased production at end of 1982.

924 Turbo 1983/4
Factory records show that no 924 Turbos were produced after 1982, but a few hundred were sold to Italy in both 1983 and 1984. It is not clear whether these were updated to current model year spec.

924 Carrera GT 1980
Internal type number 937.
European launch June 1980. Limited edition of 406 cars (incl. prototypes) of which 75 were RHD UK versions (deliveries in UK started Jan 1981).
Only differences from 1981 924 Turbo listed here.
Engine: Forged pistons, detail engine material changes. Air-to-air intercooler fitted over rocker cover. Revised turbo (see text) with max boost 0.75 bar. Repositioned oil cooler (in front of radiator). Revised exhaust. Output becomes 210 bhp at 6000 rpm, max torque 2031 lb ft at 3500 rpm.
Transmission: Gearbox Type G31/03 5-speed. Stronger final drive and shot blasted drive pinion and 3rd, 4th, 5th gears. Ratios same as G31/01 and G31/02, depending on market. 1st gear synchro from 911 for better cold changes. 911 clutch. Optional limited-slip differential.
Bodyshell: Revised front spoiler, larger rear spoiler on tailgate. Larger scoop-style intake on bonnet. Vertical slotting of front skirt replaced with single long horizontal slot at base of (flexible) front spoiler. Bonded front windshield. Flexible and flared front wings and rear wheel-arch extensions. Front/rear track becomes 1477 mm (58.2 in). Overall length 4320 mm (170.2 in) and width becomes 1735 mm (68.4 in). Height 1270 mm (50 in).
Suspension: Stronger joint shells to front steering, harder front springs (see text) and 10 mm shorter. Revised anti-roll bars (see text). Rear axle has 21 mm spacers. Strengthened rear trailing arms. Bilstein gas shock absorbers,

stiffer springs all round. Negative scrub to front axle deleted, now positive at 30 mm.
Brakes: 392 mm (11.5 in) front and 290 mm (11.4 in) rear ventilated disc with dual (divided) brake circuits front and rear. 'Stepped' tandem master cylinder. Ducting to front discs.
Wheels: Forged five-spoke (Fuchs) 7Jx15 wheels with 215/60 VR15 tyres front/rear (7/8Jx16 wheels with 225/50 VR16 rear tyres optional).
Interior: Finished in red. Wind-up windows (although UK spec cars all received power windows as standard) and Sports seats.
Weight: Prototype saved 400lb on 924 Turbo, but 'production' GT weight was 1180 kg (2602 lb) same as 924 Turbo.
Performance: Top speed 150 mph (241 km/h) 0-100 km/h (0-62 mph) in 6.9 secs. Fuel consumption claimed only a little higher than standard 924.
Price: UK £19211, incl electric windows, Panasonic radio/cassette, tinted glass, driver's door electric mirror, rear wiper, headlamp washers, sports steering wheel. Options include 7J/8J wheels/ tyre £526, detachable steel roof £339.

924 Carrera GTS
Launch January 1981
Limited edition of 59, of which up to 19 were GTR models (see below)
Engine rated at 245 bhp (DIN) at 6250 rpm with max torque 335 Nm (247 lb ft) at 3000 rpm. 8.0:1 compression ratio with turbo now set to 1.0 bar boost. 40 per cent limited-slip diff.
Suspension used cast rear trailing arms and coil springs (replacing torsion bars), 911 Turbo brakes with cross-drilled ventilated discs.
Interior is very light-weight with simple black felt trim and 935 racing seats. Sliding Resard-lined Plexiglas side windows, Plexiglas rear tailgate. Exterior has 'GTS' motif on right of panel under rear spoiler. Note custom models in text for special customers.
One piece front nose section with integrated lights and rubber over-riders eliminates front bumper entirely. No sound dampening. Weight is 1121 kg (2472 lb). 5-spoke forged alloy wheels, front 7Jx16 with 205/55 VR16 and rear 8Jx16 with 225/50 VR16. Fitted with 40 per cent limited slip differential. All models left-hand drive and finished in Guards red. Top speed is 155 mph (249 km/h) and 0-100 km/h (0-62 mph) is 6.2 seconds.

Price: West Germany DM 110,000.
           UK approx. £23950.

924 Carrera GTS Rally

Also known as GTS 'Club Sport'. Launch January 1981. Competition-ready version of GTS, with no underbody protection, and aluminium roll-over bar, Halon fire extinguisher. Body-coloured racing mirrors. Engine boosted to 280 bhp (at 1.1 bar). Fitted 8Jx16/225/50 VR16 all round. Weight was 1060 kg (2336 lb). 0-100 km/h (0-62 mph) in 5.2 secs with max speed 'over 160 mph'. Price: DM 145,000 (£31522) ex-works.

924 Carrera GTR

Launched 1981.
'Rennsport' version developed from 1980 Le Mans models, with 1.5 bar boost (7.1:1 comp. ratio) giving 375-380 bhp with max torque 405 Nm (299 lb ft) at 5600 rpm. Repositioned turbo, Kugelfischer injection and dry sump oil system. 80 per cent LSD. BBS 'Lufterflugel' 11x16 alloy wheels with Dunlop Racing front 275/600x16, rear 300/625x16 tyres. 917 brakes and weight 945 kg (2084 lb). A roll-over cage used as chassis stiffener. Cross-braced engine bay. 7.5 kg auto fire extinguisher system. 0-100 km/h (0-62 mph) in 4.7 secs with max speed 181 mph (291 km/h). Price approx. DM 180,000 (£39130) ex-works. See GTS reference concerning production numbers.

944 1982

Announced June 1981, shown Frankfurt Motor Show September 1981.
European production starts November 1981, UK launch April 1982, USA launch May 1982.
Differences listed are from 924 Carrera GT.
Chassis: 2+2 coupé bodywork entirely of hot galvanised steel with 7-year Longlife guarantee. Smooth bonnet line with no scoop and no slots in central panel between headlamps. Polyurethane front spoiler. Larger rear spoiler area.
Suspension: Double-acting hydraulic shock absorbers. Transaxle mounting redesigned for better vibration/resonance control.
Wheels: 7Jx15 pressure cast alloy (cookie cutter) with 185/70 VR15 tyres. Optional were 7Jx16 forged alloys with 205/55 VR16 tyres.
Interior: New instrument faces and revised ventilation system improving the flow of hot/cold air by 10 per cent, otherwise standard 924.
Engine: Entirely new all-aluminium four-cylinder, four-stroke in-line configuration. TOP (Thermally Optimised Porsche) combustion chamber design. Water-cooled and belt-driven overhead camshaft, with hydraulic followers. Two balance shafts to control inertial masses. Crankshaft is forged steel

in five main bearings. Lubrication by crescent-principle pump, oil cooled by oil/water heat exchanger located on exhaust side of block. Bosch L-Jetronic fuel system and Bosch Motronic (also called Digital Motor Electronics, DME system). European engine uses 98RON fuel. US versions have 3-way converter and oxygen sensor and use 91 RON unleaded fuel. Engine fitted to chassis with hydraulic mountings. Bore/stroke, 100x78.9 mm, capacity 2479 cc, compression ratio 10.6:1, (US version 9.5:1 to accommodate lead-free fuel). Oil capacity 5.5 l/5.8 US qt/1.21 Imp gal.

Output: European version:	163 bhp DIN at 5800 rpm, max torque 151 lb ft at 3000 rpm.
US version:	143 bhp SAE/150 DIN at 5500 rpm, with max torque 137 lb ft at 3000 rpm.

Electrical system: 12V 45Ah battery with 1260 watt/90 A alternator.
Gearbox: Type 016J, K 5-speed. 016J QK in Europe, RoW LSD option denoted by code 7Q. 016K QM used for USA, with optional LSD coded 8Q. In Japan the equivalent codes are QL and for LSD, 4M.

Gear	Teeth	Ratio
1	10/36	3.600:1
2	16/34	2.125:1
3	24/35	1.458:1
4	28/30	1.071:1
5	35/29 (USA: 37:27)	0.829:1 (0.730:1)
R	12/42	3.500:1
Rear axle	9/35	3.889:1

Oil volume is 2.6 litres hypoid SAE80.
Optional auto transmission. Type 087M code RCA (after October '82) for Europe, RoW. USA/Japan was type 087N code RCB (after Feb '82), shown in brackets below.

Range	Ratio
1	2.714:1 (2.552:1)
2	1.500:1 (1.448:1)
D	1.000:1 (1.000:1)
R	2.429:1 (2.462:1)
Final drive 12:37 (11:38)	3.083:1 (3.455:1)

Dimensions: Front track 1477 mm (58.2 in), rear track 1451 mm (57.1 in). Length 4200 mm (165.3 in), width 1735 mm (68.3 in), height 1275 mm (50.2 in).

Weight: DIN empty 1180 kg (2600 lb). US version, basic 1267 kg (2805 lb).

Performance

European version:	top speed 137 mph (220 km/h) with 0-100 km/h (0-62 mph) in 8.4 seconds (auto 9.6 seconds).
US version:	top speed 125 mph (201 km/h), 0-60 mph 9.0 seconds *(Road & Track)*.

Prices: UK, 944 Lux £12999, with auto £479 extra.
USA, $18450 includes 5-speed box, 4-wheel disc brakes, flush mounted front fog lamps, electric door mirrors, sunroof, air conditioning, electric antenna and tinted glass.

944 1983

Side protective strips along body. Fuel economy gauge standard. Panasonic CQ 953 radio/cassette fitted as standard on UK models with four speakers. 360 mm steering wheel now specified for UK market (was 380 mm). Power steering an option.
Prices: UK 944 Lux £13390, with auto £499 extra.

944 1984

Rear tailgate electrically released from inside. Electric tilt facility to roof panel. Options include cruise control and coloured centres to forged alloy wheel options (white, black or platinum). Vanity mirrors in both sun visors. On European models power steering still optional, but standard with auto models. Power steering and brake pad wear sensors standard on US models.
Prices: UK 944 Lux £16074, with auto £953 extra.
USA 944 basic £21440, includes air cond, sunroof, power steering, electric windows, electric door mirrors.

944 1985

Tinted glass, heated washer nozzles standard. European versions have power steering standard. Options include graduated tint to top of windshield. Optional forged wheels now available in two colours only, gold and white. New optional forged alloy front 7Jx16 wheels with 205/55 VR16 tyres and rear 8Jx16 wheels with 225/50 VR16 tyres.
In April 1985, list of 42 improvements announced for 944. Fuel tank now moulded in polyethylene allows capacity increase to 80 l/17.6 Imp gal/21.2 US gal. Active

charcoal fuel filters used in tank venting 'Oval' dash of 944 Turbo fitted, combined with 30 mm lower seat position (which has electric adjustment), 18 mm higher steering wheel. Interior ventilation improved by 35 per cent, with heating system improved. White-on-black instrumentation. Battery moves to well behind left rear wheel, fusebox and relays move to old battery position. New crankshaft, new balance shaft and modified combustion chamber. Increased oil sump capacity, larger oil pump and increased oil give 10 per cent increase in oil flow. Alternator output now 115 A, lighter, quieter starter motor. Front wishbones and rear semi-trailing arms now cast aluminium. Transaxle assembly with engine, torque tube and gearbox is attached to body at three points only to reduce noise. These improvements did not get to the UK market until the start of the 1986 model year.
Prices: UK 944 Lux £16880 with auto £627 extra.

944 1986

Improvements summarised as above plus Sekuriflex (flush fitting) bonded windshield. In UK, passenger door mirror plus Panasonic CQ 977 radio/cassette standard. Options include central locking, Sports seats with electric height adjustment and auto heating control. 7Jx15 'telephone dial' wheels with 195/65 VR15 tyres are standard.
Prices: UK 944 Lux £18234, with auto £727 extra.
USA 944 basic $22950, with auto $500 extra.

944 1987

Options available include ABS and full sports chassis (stiffer springs, shock absorbers and anti-roll bars, firmer wheel bearings and adjustment for shocks, ride height and rear anti-roll bar), plus disc-style forged alloy wheels or 7J front/8J rear x16 inch cast alloys with 205 and 225 tyres. Brake pedal effort reduced by increasing servo ratio from 3:1 to 3.4:1.
Prices: UK 944 Lux £21674, with auto £879.

944 1988

Passenger door mirror, 4 speakers and electric antenna, rear wiper, rear anti-roll bar, electric windows, cassette and coin holder, servo steering, central locking, 4-spoke 360 mm leather steering wheel, leather muffs for gear lever and handbrake standard worldwide. Headlamp beam adjustment for when fully laden and optional split rear seat backrest.
Identical performance claimed from models equipped with or without catalytic converter (but European top speed drops from 137 mph to 135 mph). Output is

PORSCHE 924

160 bhp DIN with max torque 151 lb ft and European version can be driven on unleaded fuel. Converter not fitted in UK, but Space-saver wheel now standard there. Limited edition of Zermatt silver models (30 to UK) featuring many of the popular options and 'studio' trim. These celebrate 100,000 944 models built and have multi-grey interiors, split rear seat backrest, auto heating control, sunroof with electric tilt, integral front fog lamps and the 7J/8J wider wheel fitment.

944 1989

Engine capacity increased to 2.7 litres, compression ratio increased to 10.9:1, larger inlet valves, new camshafts with new timing and revised engine management system. Output increased to 165 bhp DIN with max torque now 166 lb ft at 4200 rpm. 0-100 km/h (0-62 mph) time becomes 8.2 seconds with top speed 137 mph (220 km/h). Alarm system, armed when central locking activated, now standard. Studio cloth trims now offered for interior. Discontinued Summer 1989.

Prices: UK: 944 £25990.
             USA: $36360

944 Turbo 1985/86

Internal type number: 951
First announcement February 1985, European launch July 1985, USA launch July 1985, UK launch October 1985. Differences from mid-1985 944.
Engine: Compression ratio 8.0:1. Water cooled KKK turbocharger. External engine oil cooler. Bosch Motronic engine management with knock sensing allows use of lower octane fuel (96RON, 3 star in the UK), lead-free or leaded.
Output: 220 bhp DIN at 5800 rpm, max torque 330 Nm (243 lb ft) at 3500 rpm. Identical performance for all markets, catalytic converter not fitted outside US market.
Transmission: Stronger clutch. Gearbox oil cooler, new transmission mountings.
Suspension: 22 mm front/18 mm rear anti-roll bars (944 Sport were 21.5 mm f/14 r).
Wheels/Tyres/Brakes: 4-piston aluminium fixed-calipers with ram-air cooling to fronts. Rear axle brake balance control. 'Telephone dial' 7J front/8J rear x16 wheels with 205/55 VR16 front/225/50 VR16 rear tyres. Option is Fuchs forged alloy wheels.
Body: One-piece polyurethane front spoiler with integrated driving lamp units (no separate bumper). Flush fitted front windshield. Rear skirt fitted below rear bumper.

Interior: Boost gauge incorporated into rev-counter display (in new oval dash). Centre locking on 1986 models. Weight: 1350 kg (2977 lb) DIN empty.
Performance: top speed 152 mph (244 km/h), 0-100 km/h (0-62 mph) 6.3 seconds.
944 Turbo 'S' developed for use in US SCCA SS class racing. Adjustable koni shocks, adjustable springs, 27 mm f/21 mm r anti-roll bars with rear adjustable. Fibreglass bonnet. No electric windows, mirrors, air cond.

Prices: 944 Turbo UK £25311.
             USA $30000 approx.

944 Turbo 1987

ABS and electrically adjustable driver and passenger seats standard. Wheel rims have deeper off-sets, front axle geometry features negative-scrub and strengthened stub axles. MacPherson struts have increased diameter piston rods (these changes apply to standard 944 models fitted with ABS from this model year).
Options include electric lumbar adjustment to seats, disc forged- style alloy wheels and extended leather interior. Price: UK £32440.

944 Turbo 1988

Forged disc-style wheels standard. Space-saver standard in UK. Headlamp beam adjustment when fully laden. Options include split rear seat backrest with special rear luggage cover.
Club Sport chassis now offered as option, duplicates Turbo Cup specification with stiffer springs, shock absorbers and anti-roll bars (30 mm f/21 mm r). Adjustability for ride height, shocks and rear anti-roll bar. Also rigid attachment on rear cross tube to body, steering geometry changes towards more negative offset. Larger brake discs and calipers.
Prices: UK £36874.

944 Turbo S 1988

In UK known as 944 Turbo SE (Sport Equipment).
Limited edition of 1000 announced October 1987. Production started November 1987. Based on Turbo Cup spec, with larger turbo and boost raised from 1.75 bar to 1.82 bar and revisions to Motronic program. Output is 250 bhp DIN at 6000 rpm and 350 Nm (258 lb ft) at 4000 rpm, with 0-60 mph in 5.7 seconds and top speed of 161 mph (259 km/h). 70 RHD versions imported to UK in December 1987. Strengthened transmission with external oil cooler, standard limited slip differential. 7J front and 9J rear x16 forged disc-style

162

wheels with 225/50 VR16 front/245/45 VR16 rear tyres. All cars in Silver Rose metallic paint with 'studio' interior with burgundy cloth seat inlays and door panels. Tinted Sekuriflex laminated windshield, heated front seats and split rear seat backrest standard. Price: UK £41249.

944 Turbo 1989
Directly based on Turbo Cup-derived 944 Turbo SE, with same 250 bhp output. Only 944 Turbo available for 1989 year. Alarm system now standard on UK cars. USA spec cars still as 1988 base model.
Price: UK £39892.

944 Turbo 1990
'Wing' rear spoiler fitted, plus 7.5Jx16 front wheels. UK models now have 3-way catalytic converter standard. Base model dropped in USA (only Turbo S available).

Prices: UK £42296
        USA $48060

944S 1986/7
Announced July 1986, launched Europe/USA August 1986, launched UK September 1986.
Differences are from 1987 944.
Engine: water-cooled, four-cylinder, twin-overhead camshaft configuration. 4-valves per cylinder, twin overhead camshafts with new wider/stronger toothed belt drive. New intake manifold with magnesium passages, new exhaust system, oil sump and re-programmed digital electronics with three sensor knock detection system. Compression ratio 10.9:1.
Output 190 bhp DIN at 6000 rpm, max torque 170 lb ft at 4300 rpm. Rev limit increased from 6500 rpm to 6800 rpm. Fuel 95 RON, unleaded possible.
Transmission: New gear ratios, but same worldwide.
Suspension: Upgraded wheel bearing pivots and larger pistons for front shock absorbers. Rear wheel brake circuit fitted with brake pressure regulator to prevent wheel locking under severe conditions. Club Sport suspension and lightening option available (see 944 Turbo for spec).
Body: Externally distinguishable from 944 only by small (and optional) '16 ventiler' badges on the left of the panel beneath the rear window and on the sides behind the repeater lights. Also '944S' badge on right of panel below rear window. Air bag safety system optional in US.
Weight: 1280 kg (2822 lb) DIN.
Performance: Top speed 142 mph (228 km/h) and 0-100 km/h 0-62 mph 7.9 seconds.
Price: UK £23997.

944S 1988
Differences from 1988 944. Rear underbody spoiler standard.   Price: UK £25149.

944S2 1989
Production starts Feb 1989.
Engine now increased to 3 litres capacity. Bore/Stroke is 104x88 mm giving a capacity of 2990 cc (182.2 cu in). Entirely new crankcase (4.5 kg lighter, with reduced coolant capacity, siamesed cylinders and anti-oil foaming technology). Plastic sump moulding. 'Quadrilateral' air intake system for optimum response, revised electronics programme with semi-intelligence in knock-sensing, external oil cooler and engine compartment ventilation with three-stage fan. Output is 211 bhp DIN at 5800 rpm with or without converter. Torque is 280 Nm (207 lb ft) at 4100 rpm. Fuel 91 RON, unleaded.
Weight: 1310 kg (2888 lb) DIN.
Transmission: Gearbox, drive shafts strengthened.
Wheels/Brakes: 4-piston calipers/discs from Turbo, forced air cooling. Turbo shock absorbers, anti-roll bars and suspension. 7Jf/8Jr wheels with 205/55 and 225/50 ZR16 tyres.
Exterior: As 944 Turbo, with integrated front polyurethane nose section and underbody covers.
Performance: Top speed 149 mph (240 km/h) and 0-100 km/h (0-62 mph) in 7.1 seconds. (Note: Road & Track achieved 0-60 mph in 6.4 seconds).

Price: UK £31304.
USA. $45598.

944S2 1990
UK models fitted with 3-way catalytic converter.
Prices: UK £33963
        USA $42515

944S2 Cabriolet 1989/90
Announced as design study Frankfurt Show 1985. Start of production March/April 1989. Worldwide deliveries commenced from Summer 1989. Sub-contracted cabriolet conversion by American Sunroof Company at Heilbron, West Germany. Empty weight 1390 kg (3058 lb), Coupé is 1340 kg (3058 lb); Coupé is 1340 kg) (2948 lb). Extra weight comes from Porsche-fitted additional floor pan member, front and rear door jam braces and floor pan crossmembers. Windshield shortened by 60 mm and raked back 14 mm. Revised side windows. Roof operation is semi-automatic (requires manual release). Electric operation is only an option in certain markets, (but not UK or USA). Rear luggage space significantly reduced by cabrio storage area. Deleted rear spoiler, rear wiper and heated window.

Price: UK £36713 (Panasonic CQ F35) 1990: £38935
      USA $48600 (Blaupunkt Reno)

A P P E N D I X 2

Chassis and Engine Numbering Methodology

924/924 Turbo/Carrera GT Chassis Numbers

From 1977 to 1979 924 chassis numbers were ten digits, structured as follows:

Type	Model Year	Version	Serial No
924	7	1	00001-on

Versions: 1 = Europe; 2 = USA, California; 3 = Japan. In 1979 the 924 Turbo chassis were given the version number 4 (for Europe, RoW) and 5 (for USA, Japan).

European Economic Community and USA legislation precipitated a change in the chassis numbering system necessary for 1980. From 1981 chassis would be identifiable on a worldwide basis for a period of 30 years by a 17 digit system. For 1980, a preliminary ten digit system was used, which was also carried over to the CGT and GTS/R:

Type 924:	Model Year	Plant code	Vehicle Type	Engine Type	Serial No
92	A	0	4	1	0001-on
924 Turbo:					
93	A	0	1	4	0001-on
Carrera:					
93	B	N	7	0	0001-on

(Serial numbers for CGT were 0001 to 0006 (Weissach built prototypes), and 0051 to 0450, Neckarsulm built series of 400).

Carrera GTS					
93	B	N	7	1	0 001 to 0050

Note that the 1980 model year was coded A, 1981 was B and so on and plant code 'N' denoted Neckarsulm. From 1981, the volume model numbers became:

World Make Code	VSD Code USA	Veh. type	Test No	Model Year	Manuf locat	Veh. Type	Body/engine Code	Serial No
WPO	ZZZ	92	Z	B	N	4	5	0001-on

1982-1985.
Model year codes as follows: 1982 = C, 1983 = D, 1984 = E, 1985 = F.

924/924 Turbo/Carrera GT Engine Numbers

Note each engine code followed by continuous 6-digit serial number, regardless of model year.

Year	Code letters (Engine Type)
1977	XK = Europe, RoW
	XH = USA/Canada
	XF = California, Japan
1978	XK = Europe, RoW
	XJ = Europe, RoW – RHD
	XG = USA
	XE = California
	XG = Japan
1979	924 as 1978
	3101 = Turbo, Europe, RoW
	3102 = Turbo, USA/Cal/Jap.
1980	XK = Europe, RoW – LHD
	XJ = Europe, RoW – RHD
	VC = USA/Calif/Can/Jap.
1981	Engine numbers as 1980, plus:
	3103 = Turbo Srs 2; Europe, RoW (LHD & RHD)
	3150 = CGT; Europe, RoW (LHD & RHD)
	3104 = Turbo Srs 2: USA, Calif/Canada, Japan
1982	As 1981, but less CGT
1983-5	As 1982, but less 924 Turbo
1986	For the 924S, engine numbers were as follows (with the G designation marking the 1986 model year).
	43G 00001 – 60000 = Europe, RoW manual
	43G 60001 – 90000 = Europe, RoW auto

944 Chassis Numbers

1983, (D programme) as 924 except that: WPO ZZZ 94 Z D N 4 00001-49999 for Europe, RoW.
WPO AAO 94 0 D N 4 50001-99999 for USA/Canada.
1984 to date, change model year letter as follows: 1984 = E, 1985 = F, 1986 = G, 1987 = H, 1988 = I, 1989 = J.
944 Turbo chassis numbering same as 944, except model type is 951. This shown in digits 7, 8 and 12 of the number, e.g.:
WPO ZZZ 95 Z G N 1 00001-49999 is a Europe, RoW 1986 model year sequence. WPO AAO 95 O G N 1 50001-99999 is a USA/Canada 1986 model sequence.
944S chassis numbers are identical to 944 except that serial numbers were allocated as follows:

944S	00001-19999 Europe, RoW, Japan
	1987: 50001-59999 USA, Canada
	1988: 70001-79999 USA, Canada
	1988: 80001-89999 Sports package worldwide

944 Engine Numbers

1983:	41D 0001–4999	944 Europe, RoW
	5001–9999	ditto, auto

Serial numbers included expander numbers A000-A999, B0002-B999, and so on to letter H.

PORSCHE 924

	43D 0001–4999	944 USA, Japan
	5001–9999	ditto, auto
1984:	41E 00001–20000	944 Europe, RoW
	41E 20001–30000	ditto, auto
	43E 00001–20000	944 USA, Japan, Canada
	43E 20001–30000	ditto, auto

1985: As 1984 with 'F' year designation and expanded serial number ranges to 60000.

1986:	41G 00001–20000	944 Europe, RoW
	41G 20001–30000	ditto, auto
	43G 00001–60000	944 USA, Canada, Japan, Australia
	43G 60001–90000	ditto, auto
	44G 0001–00320	944 Turbo, Europe, RoW
	45G 0001–20000	944 Turbo, Worldwide

1987:	944: As 1986, with model year letter changed to "H".
	944 Turbo: All markets now 45H 00001–10000.
	944S: 42H 00001–60000 all markets.

1988:	46J 00001–60000	944 Worldwide
	46J 60001–70000	ditto, auto
	42J 00001–50000	944S worldwide
	45J 00001–10000	944 Turbo worldwide

A P P E N D I X 3

PRODUCTION VOLUME DATA

Model	Year	No. Produced
924	1976	19168
	1977	21956
	1978	22068
	1979	15690
	1980	11908
	1981	14183
	1982	5955
	1983	5887
	1984	3170
	1985	2319
924 total		**122304**
924 Turbo	1978	86
	1979	5023
	1980	3044
	1981	3578
	1982	444
	1983	210
924 Turbo total		**12385**
924 Carrera GT	1980	**406***

*This figure includes prototypes
924 Carrera GTS
1981 **59***
(* of which up to 19 were GTR)

(Supplied to all markets – note these are not sales figures)

Model	Year	No. Produced
924S	1985	1689
	1986	6844
	1987	6868
	1988	881*
924S total		**16282**

*924S production ceased Sept 1988

Model	Year	No. Produced
944	1981	43
	1982	13873
	1983	24761
	1984	24455
	1985	24651
	1986	11816
	1987	10807
	1988*	3660
944 total		**114066**
944 Turbo	1984	49
	1985	4790
	1986	8263
	1987	5059
	1988*	2888
944 Turbo total		**21049**

Model	Year	No. Produced
944S	1986	3861
	1987	3099
	1988*	614
944S total		**7574**

*1988 volumes are to the end of November only.

A P P E N D I X   4

Clubs
and contacts

Clubs

Listed below are the major Porsche Clubs in the English-speaking world. Should you wish to know the address of any other Porsche Club in any other country write to the Porsche Clubs Co-ordinator, Dr.Ing.h.c.F.Porsche A.G., Porschestrasses 15-19, D-7140 Ludwigsberg, West Germany.

AUSTRALIA: Porsche Club New South Wales: PO Box 183, Lindfield, NSW 2070, Sydney, Australia.

Porsche Club Victoria; PO Box 222, Kew, Victoria, 3101, Australia.

Porsche Club Queensland; PO Box 584, Brisbane 4001, Australia.

Porsche Club Western Australia, PO Box 447, South Perth 6151, Western Australia.

GREAT BRITAIN: Porsche Club Great Britain, Ayton House, West End, Northleach, Glos, GL54 3HG, England. Tel: 0451 60792.

PCGB Motor Sport Division, Doric House, 56 Alcester Rd., Studley, Warwickshire, B80 7LG. Tel: 052785 4108, Fax: 052785 2746.

The PCGB is the second largest Porsche club in the world. They enjoy close relations with the factory in Stuttgart.

The PCGB organise a variety of events each year on a national and regional basis to suit all tastes. These include what must be the strongest club one-make motor sport activity worldwide, dinner dances, pub nights, factory visits and driving tuition events. There is an annual Concours d'Elégance and the club receives numerous invitations to attend international Porsche activities overseas. By 1990, the PCGB numbered over 8,000 members and was divided into 29 regions (including one in the United Arab Emirates!). Members can participate in any event, local or national.

The Club produces an impressive glossy magazine *Porsche Post* free to members every two months. Club insignia is available at reasonable cost, together with free technical advice, workshop equipment and manuals. The Club has obtained parts discounts from many Official Porsche Centres in the UK.

HONG KONG: Porsche Club Hong Kong, No. 1 Yip Fat Street, PO Box 24539, Aberdeen, Hong Kong.

NEW ZEALAND: Porsche Club New Zealand, PO Box 39-074, Auckland 9, New Zealand.

UNITED STATES: Porsche Club of America, PO Box 10402, Alexandria, VA 22310, USA.

The largest Porsche Club in the world, the PCA is divided into 126 chartered regions. Events are organised on a national and regional basis, with the annual 'Porsche Parade', lasting nearly a week, being the most important. The Club sends *Porsche Panorama* monthly to its members free and each region usually has its own newsletter.

Official Porsche Sales Organisations

Porsche Cars Great Britain Ltd, Bath Rd., Calcot, Reading, Berks, RG3 7SE for a list of the UK Official Porsche Centres.

Porsche Cars North America Inc., PO Box 30911, Reno, NV 89520, for a listing of all Official Porsche Centres in the USA.

UK Porsche Specialists Assisting in the Preparation of this Book

AUTOFARM LTD, London Rd., Cow Roast, Nr. Tring, Herts, HP23 5RE. Tel: 0442 890911

CLUB AUTOMOBILE SERVICES, 6 Park Lane, Cradley Heath, Halesowen, West Midlands, B63 2QY. Tel: 0384 410879.

PICKUP, LEASK LTD, 59, Maygrove Rd., West Hampstead, london, NW6 2EE. Tel: 01 435 8435

TEMPO RACING DEVELOPMENTS, Unit E2, Bedfont Trading Estate, Feltham, Middx. Tel: 01 890 1506

CHRIS TURNER PORSCHE, Unit 49, Sapcote Trading Estate, 374 High Rd., Willesden, London, NW10. 01 451 6000

Use of English

As this book has been written in England, it uses the appropriate English component names, phrases, and spelling. Some of these differ from those used in America. Normally, these cause no difficulty, but to make sure, a glossary is printed below. In ordering spare parts remember the parts list may use some of these words:

English	American	English	American
Accelerator	Gas pedal	Locks	Latches
Aerial	Antenna	Methylated spirit	Denatured alcohol
Anti-roll bar	Stabiliser or sway bar	Motorway	Freeway, turnpike etc
Big-end bearing	Rod bearing	Number plate	License plate
Bonnet (engine cover)	Hood	Paraffin	Kerosene
Boot (luggage compartment)	Trunk	Petrol	Gasoline (gas)
Bulkhead	Firewall	Petrol tank	Gas tank
Bush	Bushing	'Pinking'	'Pinging'
Cam follower or tappet	Valve lifter or tappet	Prise (force apart)	Pry
Carburettor	Carburetor	Propeller shaft	Driveshaft
Catch	Latch	Quarterlight	Quarter window
Choke/venturi	Barrel	Retread	Recap
Circlip	Snap-ring	Reverse	Back-up
Clearance	Lash	Rocker cover	Valve cover
Crownwheel	Ring gear (of differential)	Saloon	Sedan
Damper	Shock absorber, shock	Seized	Frozen
Disc (brake)	Rotor/disk	Sidelight	Parking light
Distance piece	Spacer	Silencer	Muffler
Drop arm	Pitman arm	Sill panel (beneath doors)	Rocker panel
Drop head coupe	Convertible	Small end, little end	Piston pin or wrist pin
Dynamo	Generator (DC)	Spanner	Wrench
Earth (electrical)	Ground	Split cotter (for valve spring cap)	Lock (for valve spring retainer)
Engineer's blue	Prussian blue	Split pin	Cotter pin
Estate car	Station wagon	Steering arm	Spindle arm
Exhaust manifold	Header	Sump	Oil pan
Fault finding/diagnosis	Troubleshooting	Swarf	Metal chips or debris
Float chamber	Float bowl	Tab washer	Tang or lock
Free-play	Lash	Tappet	Valve lifter
Freewheel	Coast	Thrust bearing	Throw-out bearing
Gearbox	Transmission	Top gear	High
Gearchange	Shift	Torch	Flashlight
Grub screw	Setscrew, Allen screw	Trackrod (of steering)	Tie-rod (or connecting rod)
Gudgeon pin	Piston pin or wrist pin	Trailing shoe (of brake)	Secondary shoe
Halfshaft	Axleshaft	Transmission	Whole drive line
Handbrake	Parking brake	Tyre	Tire
Hood	Soft top	Van	Panel wagon/van
Hot spot	Heat riser	Vice	Vise
Indicator	Turn signal	Wheel nut	Lug nut
Interior light	Dome lamp	Windscreen	Windshield
Layshaft (of gearbox)	Countershaft	Wing/mudguard	Fender
Leading shoe (of brake)	Primary shoe		

Professional motor mechanics are trained in safe working procedures. However enthusiastic you may be about getting on with the job in hand, do take the time to ensure that your safety is not put at risk. A moment's lack of attention can result in an accident, as can failure to observe certain elementary precautions.

There will always be new ways of having accidents, and the following points do not pretend to be a comprehensive list of all dangers; they are intended rather to make you aware of the risks and to encourage a safety-conscious approach to all work you carry out on your vehicle.

Essential DOs and DON'Ts

DON'T rely on a single jack when working underneath the vehicle. Always use reliable additional means of support, such as axle stands, securely placed under a part of the vehicle that you know will not give way.

DON'T attempt to loosen or tighten high-torque nuts (e.g. wheel hub nuts) while the vehicle is on a jack; it may be pulled off.

DON'T start the engine without first ascertaining that the transmission is in neutral (or 'Park' where applicable) and the parking brake applied.

DON'T suddenly remove the filler cap from a hot cooling system – cover it with a cloth and release the pressure gradually first, or you may get scalded by escaping coolant.

DON'T attempt to drain oil until you are sure it has cooled sufficiently to avoid scalding you.

DON'T grasp any part of the engine, exhaust or catalytic converter without first ascertaining that it is sufficiently cool to avoid burning you.

DON'T allow brake fluid or antifreeze to contact vehicle paintwork.

DON'T syphon toxic liquids such as fuel, brake fluid or antifreeze by mouth, or allow them to remain on your skin.

DON'T inhale dust – it may be injurious to health (see *Asbestos* below).

DON'T allow any spilt oil or grease to remain on the floor – wipe it up straight away, before someone slips on it.

DON'T use ill-fitting spanners or other tools which may slip and cause injury.

DON'T attempt to lift a heavy component which may be beyond your capability – get assistance.

DON'T rush to finish a job, or take unverified short cuts.

DON'T allow children or animals in or around an unattended vehicle.

DO wear eye protection when using power tools such as drill, sander, bench grinder etc, and when working under the vehicle.

DO use a barrier cream on your hands prior to undertaking dirty jobs – it will protect your skin from infection as well as making the dirt easier to remove afterwards; but make sure your hands aren't left slippery. Note that long-term contact with used engine oil can be a health hazard.

DO keep loose clothing (cuffs, tie etc) and long hair well out of the way of moving mechanical parts.

DO remove rings, wristwatch etc, before working on the vehicle – especially the electrical system.

DO ensure that any lifting tackle used has a safe working load rating adequate for the job.

DO keep your work area tidy – it is only too easy to fall over articles left lying around.

DO get someone to check periodically that all is well, when working alone on the vehicle.

DO carry out work in a logical sequence and check that everything is correctly assembled and tightened afterwards.

DO remember that your vehicle's safety affects that of yourself and others. If in doubt on any point, get specialist advice.

IF, in spite of following these precautions, you are unfortunate enough to injure yourself, seek medical attention as soon as possible.

Asbestos

Certain friction, insulating, sealing, and other products – such as brake linings, brake bands, clutch linings, torque converters, gaskets, etc – contain asbestos. *Extreme care must be taken to avoid inhalation of dust from such products since it is hazardous to health*. If in doubt, assume that they *do* contain asbestos.

Fire

Remember at all times that petrol (gasoline) is highly flammable. Never smoke, or have any kind of naked flame around, when working on the vehicle. But the risk does not end there – a spark caused by an electrical short-circuit, by two metal surfaces contacting each other, by careless use of tools, or even by static electricity built up in your body under certain conditions, can ignite petrol vapour, which in a confined space is highly explosive.

Always disconnect the battery earth (ground) terminal before working on any part of the fuel or electrical system, and never risk spilling fuel on to a hot engine or exhaust.

It is recommended that a fire extinguisher of a type suitable for fuel and electrical fires is kept handy in the garage or workplace at all times.

Never try to extinguish a fuel or electrical fire with water.

Note: *Any reference to a 'torch' appearing in this manual should always be taken to mean a hand-held battery-operated electric lamp or flashlight. It does NOT mean a welding/gas torch or blowlamp.*

Fumes

Certain fumes are highly toxic and can quickly cause unconsciousness and even death if inhaled to any extent. Petrol (gasoline) vapour comes into this category, as do the vapours from certain solvents such as trichloroethylene. Any draining or pouring of such volatile fluids should be done in a well ventilated area.

When using cleaning fluids and solvents, read the instructions carefully. Never use materials from unmarked containers – they may give off poisonous vapours.

Never run the engine of a motor vehicle in an enclosed space such as a garage. Exhaust fumes contain carbon monoxide which is extremely poisonous; if you need to run the engine, always do so in the open air or at least have the rear of the vehicle outside the workplace.

If you are fortunate enough to have the use of an inspection pit, never drain or pour petrol, and never run the engine, while the vehicle is standing over it; the fumes, being heavier than air, will concentrate in the pit with possibly lethal results.

The battery

Never cause a spark, or allow a naked light, near the vehicle's battery. It will normally be giving off a certain amount of hydrogen gas, which is highly explosive.

Always disconnect the battery earth (ground) terminal before working on the fuel or electrical systems.

If possible, loosen the filler plugs or cover when charging the battery from an external source. Do not charge at an excessive rate or the battery may burst.

Take care when topping up and when carrying the battery. The acid electrolyte, even when diluted, is very corrosive and should not be allowed to contact the eyes or skin.

If you ever need to prepare electrolyte yourself, always add the acid slowly to the water, and never the other way round. Protect against splashes by wearing rubber gloves and goggles.

When jump starting a car using a booster battery, for negative earth (ground) vehicles, connect the jump leads in the following sequence: First connect one jump lead between the positive (+) terminals of the two batteries. Then connect the other jump lead first to the negative (–) terminal of the booster battery, and then to a good earthing (ground) point on the vehicle to be started, at least 18 in (45 cm) from the battery if possible. Ensure that hands and jump leads are clear of any moving parts, and that the two vehicles do not touch. Disconnect the leads in the reverse order.

Mains electricity and electrical equipment

When using an electric power tool, inspection light etc, always ensure that the appliance is correctly connected to its plug and that, where necessary, it is properly earthed (grounded). Do not use such appliances in damp conditions and, again, beware of creating a spark or applying excessive heat in the vicinity of fuel or fuel vapour. Also ensure that the appliances meet the relevant national safety standards.

Ignition HT voltage

A severe electric shock can result from touching certain parts of the ignition system, such as the HT leads, when the engine is running or being cranked, particularly if components are damp or the insulation is defective. Where an electronic ignition system is fitted, the HT voltage is much higher and could prove fatal.

INDEX

172